Handbook for Multisensory Worship, Volume 2

Handbook for Multisensory Worship, Volume 2

**Kim Miller
and the Ginghamsburg Church Worship Team**

**Abingdon Press
Nashville**

HANDBOOK FOR MULTISENSORY WORSHIP, VOLUME 2

ISBN 0-687-05203-3

Scripture taken from *THE MESSAGE*. Copyright © by Eugene H. Peterson, 1993, 1994, 1995. Used by permission of NavPress Publishing Group.

Scripture quotations noted NIV are taken from the *Holy Bible: New International Version*. Copyright © 1973, 1978, 1984 by the International Bible Society. Used by permission of Zondervan Bible Publishers.

Acknowledgement is made for permission to excerpt the following material:

"The Magna Carta of Trust" from *A Cup of Coffee at the Soul Café* by Leonard Sweet with Denise Marie Sino. Copyright © 1998 by Broadman & Holman Publishers, Nashville, Tennessee. Used by permission.

Adaptations of "Psalm 51" and "Psalm 72" from *Psalms/Now* by Leslie F. Brandt. Copyright © 1973 by Concordia Publishing House, St. Louis, Missouri. Used by permission.

"Cats in the Cradle," Words and music by Harry Chapin and Sandy Chapin. Copyright © 1974 Story Songs, Ltd. International Copyright Secured. All Rights Reserved. Used by permission.

Cataloging-in-Publication data is available from the Library of Congress.

Contents

Foreword

I love searching for lost things. While others may be frustrated by the thought of loss, I love the possibility of turning over that last stone and discovering what was missing. Whether I'm searching for a piece of jewelry, a glove, a quote from a book, or my car in a parking lot; I find the thrill of the hunt to be a powerful motivating force.

Jesus was greatly concerned about lost things—coins, sheep, children, and people. Jesus gave his followers permission to leave the 99, if need be, and go find the one that is lost, because bottom line, lost people matter to God. In the pages of this handbook, you will find an innovative approach to planning worship celebrations that invite lost people to Jesus. For those who are already connected to God, these celebrations will draw them into a closer relationship with Jesus the Savior, the one who cares about their unique lives, and who is now present among us in the form of the Holy Spirit.

Multisensory worship is defined not by our distinctions; that is, not by traditional, contemporary, seeker-sensitive, and so forth, but by our common thread of humanness. We are all humans who see, feel, taste, touch, and smell. People don't need great explanations about God so much as tangible experiences of a loving God.

The Church is truly an ancient-future church. Stained glass and media screens. Candles and stage lights. Saints and sinners. Secular and sacred. Young and old. Believers and seekers together. We believe it's more about asking the right questions than giving the right answers. Multisensory churches seek to tell the gospel in a language our world can understand.

As stated in the first *Handbook for Multisensory Worship*, we believe that each faith community and its weekly worship event will be a unique demonstration of God's Kingdom here on earth. Feel free to use from these pages whatever works in your own setting. Becoming familiar with the segments may spawn new, more powerful ideas that can be developed in your own celebrations. If you are a new or smaller congregation however, you may enjoy the benefit of occasionally having an entire worship event mapped out for you. Remember, this is a handbook; use it as a resource to support what God is creating in your midst. And if appropriate for your situation, the corresponding graphics for these celebrations are available online for purchase.

Whatever your unique situation, may God be powerfully present as you set out to do the mission of Jesus, to reach the lost and to set the oppressed free in your corner of the world.

Creatively yours,
Kim Miller
& the Ginghamsburg Worship Team

Introduction

How to Use This Book

Worship celebrations that are designed to speak to the present culture must be planned for the purpose of connecting people to God and their God-destiny. That's why we developed a format for *why* we put a celebration together before we plan *how* we will do it. The format includes these elements:

Word: The Word of God, brought to the team by the speaker

Felt Need: The presenting need(s) that the people bring to worship surrounding the given theme or words

Desired Outcome: The targeted responses toward which the worshippers will be challenged

Theme: The "package" in which the message is wrapped, a catchy title to sum up the whole

Metaphor and Look: A visual representation of the message to be communicated

Structure: The actual order of worship

When planning our weekly event, we discipline ourselves as a team to explore thoroughly the first five elements before proceeding with the creative structure itself. This list becomes a map whereby the team can stay on its course.

Music

The song suggestions are from a wide variety of sources. For popular secular songs (featured or opening music) our bandleaders generally find the appropriate audio CD at a retail store or in our own CD libraries. They listen to the music on the recording and write arrangements for the band members. (These arrangements are meant for performance only.) Your local audio CD store is a great resource, and their employees can assist in finding the CD by using the artist's name as a reference. Many retailers use a music database and can identify a CD that may have a particular song on it. In addition, you can do an artist search on the Web by going to the individual artist's site. This may be helpful in locating a particular song and lyrics. We do change some of the words now and then to suit our own performance purposes. Of course, the performance on a copywritten song must be limited to the live performance in worship only. We cannot record, sell, or reproduce the songs in any way without further permission (see copyright laws below).

The musical selections in the Song Celebration segments are those that the entire congregation sings together. We can't promise that they are available at this time, but the possible resources are listed in this handbook. These publishers generally offer written music as well as a recorded version.

Media

A thumbnail image of the main graphic that depicts the metaphor for the celebrations can be seen at the top of the page beginning each new celebration. These graphics are available for purchase via download from the digital store at (http://www.ginghamsburg.org). Some celebrations offer more than one usable graphic like a background on which you can put scriptures or song text, or perhaps a graphic that already includes text.

Some video products are available through www.ginghamsburg.org. The Ginghamsburg video collection known as *The Visual Edge* is available from www.cokesbury.com. In addition to the basic use of media each week, we produce our own "spots" to showcase various ministries or to tell someone's personal story. Since these pieces would not be applicable to other congregations, we encourage churches to produce their own spots. Video clips from rented or purchased videos can also be used to support the theme or message in some way. Throughout the book, we have provided suggestions for video clips and described the scene to be used. The basic applicable legal code is found under Section 110 of the Copyright Law of 1976 (17 U.S.C. & 110 (3)). Section 110 states that, without fear of breaking the law, churches may:

—Perform nondramatic literary or musical works and religious dramatic and musical works, or

—Display individual works of a nonsequential nature (17 U.S.C. & 101)

during services at a house of worship or other religious assembly. *Display*, as defined in legalese, means to "show a copy of [a work] either directly or by means of a film, slide, television image, or any other device or process or, in the case of a motion picture or other audiovisual work, to show individual images nonsequentially."

In other words, this means churches may:

—Perform contemporary songs, regardless of the owner/writer;

—Show still images regardless of their sources, and even show frames of a film if they are not in sequence.

For further legal information regarding copyright and reproduction of music, please contact your own lawyer, or consider purchasing a copy of Len Wilson's book, *The Wired Church*.

Most of the scripts for the Calls to Worship, Prayers, Dramas, and main graphic images are included; however, a few are not available at this time, due to copyright issues. Consider this your opportunity to write and add some pieces on your own! We also encourage you to experiment with the visual enhancement, and find what works best in your particular setting. Always plan visual enhancement with safety in mind. Candles are wonderful symbols, but caution should be exercised when people are close by. Check and double check that lights and candles are out when the building is vacated.

Writing this resource for other churches was a wonderful next-step for us. It is our hope, however, that as you gather ideas, you will also catch a glimpse of what a team can design together in the power of God's Spirit. We anticipate that your team will discover its own amazing potential to present the timeless story of God's love for humankind.

Celebration

1

Stop, Look, & See

Stop, Look, & See

Felt Need: The busyness of our activity distracts us from the joy of each moment with God and others

Desired Outcome: To change our priorities in order to live out what God has presented as most important

Theme: Stop, Look, and See

Word: Psalm 46:10

Metaphor/Image: Clocks

The Lesson: Life can get going so fast that we never settle our spirits enough to enjoy the moment, to celebrate the lives that connect with our own. This worship experience reminds us of the miracles set before us each day. Participants will come away with a renewed call to making each moment count.

The Look: Because the drama "Cats In the Cradle" is central to this celebration, we allowed the drama set to establish a unique appearance. We used a large brown leather chair, a table with photo album, phone, and a lamp. Leave the lamp lit (with a low watt bulb) throughout the celebration. The lamp-post from the Call to Worship can be positioned on the other side of the stage.

Featured Option: New Members

Worship Celebration

Opening Music

Singer   **"Feelin' Groovy"**

Singer sits under lamppost, playing guitar and singing song.

Call to Worship

Host

Light speaker only; project if possible or show a main graphic on cue(*).
Host interrupts singer; continue lighting them.
Project host and singer, then go to main graphic.

Host interrupts singer and speaks sideways to him:

Host: Whoooooooooaaaaaaaaa. Cut! It's all fine and good to sing nice songs, but who on earth has time to slow down? Rather idealistic, don't you think? Hello lamppost? Come on, I barely have time to talk to my wife, let alone inanimate street objects! Let's get real here.... *(turns to speak to audience)* Do you suppose God knew what our situation would be when he gave this direction in the Bible?

Singer: *(singing)* Be still and know that I am God.
This is the day I have made. Have joy and gladness right now.

Host: Too often I think of happiness as something in the past or as an opportunity in the future. How often do I miss today as I hurry to stand in line for tomorrow?

We are challenged to *stop, look, and see what God is doing right now. To slow down, because we move too fast to experience all God offers. Stand with us now as we celebrate this moment with our Creator.

Song Celebration

Band   **"God Is So Good"**
"New Song Arisin'"
"Oh Lord, You're Beautiful"

Lights up on band; project words.

Affirmation of New Members   **"Oh Lord, You're Beautiful"**

Ask participants come to the front during the second verse of "Oh Lord, You're Beautiful." Have host introduce and explain the welcoming of new members by baptism or reaffirmation (see below). Play soft music under. Participants are reaffirmed or baptized (resume singing). Host asks questions of all, then prays (soft music only). New members return to seats (resume singing).

This special group of people assembled before us today has recently completed a three-month commitment in which they've gained a wealth of knowledge, been challenged in their Christian journey, and grown closer to Jesus Christ.

Baptism is the public statement of a person's relationship with Jesus, a statement that they will not live for themselves but will totally surrender and sell out to Jesus, by choosing a lifestyle that reflects and demonstrates Jesus' life. Part of this group made the decision to be baptized today or, if they've been baptized previously, to have the vows taken at their baptism reaffirmed. Let us sing to God as we rejoice because of these brothers and sisters.

Participants are baptized or reaffirmed; resume singing "Oh Lord, You're Beautiful." Host asks questions of group; play music softly in background.

You have completed the process of preparation! You have studied together, socialized together, gotten to know each other. You have come to an understanding of the meaning of membership at (*name of church*). Now you are indicating your readiness to join this community of faith at a deeper level.

By answering the following questions, you are sharing the commitments you are making with the entire congregation.

> 1. Have you accepted Jesus Christ as your personal Lord and Savior? (Yes)
> 2. Do you believe in the Christian faith as contained in the Old and New Testaments? (Yes)
> 3. Do you covenant to be a faithful member of Christ's church and to live a lifestyle honoring God? (Yes)
> 4. Will you uphold (*name of church*) with your prayers, presence, resources, and participation in ministry? (Yes)

(*Clapping*) Let's welcome these new members to the (*name of church*) family.

Offering and Announcements

Host

Light host; project host intermittently with graphics.

We give this morning as an act of worship. Will the ushers please come to receive our offerings? We welcome each of you here today, and if this would be one of your first times to visit, please be sure to stop by the information desk for an information packet.

Video Clip

from *Hook*

_____

Lower house lights. Host introduces clip. This is the scene where Grandma Wendy asks Peter (in front hallway of her home) "what is so terribly important about your terribly important life?"

Featured Music, Drama, Prayer

Host, Band, and Actors   "Cats in the Cradle"

_____

Light host, band, and drama area. Host will introduce drama and lead prayer after closing; have band softly play song.

We spend our todays grasping for more successful tomorrows. But when tomorrow comes, we don't even recognize it. It looks like another today that we need to get through. Living in any other time but the "here and now" is a perfect recipe for broken relationships and unfulfilled hopes. This story could be any of us. *(Singing begins.)*

"Cats in the Cradle"

A man is seated onstage. He is nicely dressed and has a briefcase close by. As lights come up he spots a photo album on the table, picks it up, and thoughtfully begins turning the pages. If possible, project pictures from the photo album onscreen.

Band: **My child arrived just the other day.**
He came to the world in the usual way.
But there were planes to catch, and bills to pay.
He learned to walk while I was away.

The man slowly shakes his head from side to side. He is engrossed in the pictures.

Band: **And he was talkin 'fore I knew it, and as he grew,**
He'd say,"I'm gonna be like you, Dad.
You know I'm gonna be like you."

The man smiles and laughs a bit, continuing to look at the album.

Band (*Chorus*): **And the cat's in the cradle and the silver spoon,**
Little boy blue and the man in the moon.
When you coming home, Dad? "I don't know when,
But we'll get together then, yeah.
You know we'll have a good time then."

A young boy enters wearing a ball cap backward, carrying a wooden bat and an imaginary ball. The man remains on the chair as though daydreaming. The boy catches his eye and the man is taken up in the moment, watching.

Band: **My son turned ten just the other day.**
He said, "Thanks for the ball, Dad, come on let's play.
Can you teach me to throw? I said. "Not today,
I got a lot to do. He said, "That's OK."

The boy motions with his ball as if questioning to the man. He then encounters rejection and puts his head down in sadness. He exits, stopping to look back and adjust his cap, casting one hopeful glance back at his dad.

As he exits the man reaches toward him, then shakes his head and goes back to the album.

Band: **And he walked away, but his smile, lemme tell you,**
Said, "I'm gonna be like him, yeah.
You know I'm gonna be like him."

And the cat's in the cradle and the silver spoon,
Little boy blue and the man in the moon.
"When you coming home Dad?" "I don't know when,
But we'll get together then,
You know we'll have a good time then."

A young man bounds up to the extension, a grown and matured version of the young boy. He acknowledges the man from a distance with some reserve.

Band: **Well, he came from college just the other day,**
So much like a man I just had to say,
"Son, I'm proud of you. Can you sit for a while?"
He shook his head, and he said with a smile . . .

The man is excited and motions for his son to come sit in the other chair.

Band: **"What I'd really like Dad, is to borrow the car keys.**
See you later. Can I have them please?"

More animated, the son wishes to skip the small talk, reaches in his pocket and pulls out a set of keys, throws them up, catches them, and waves good-bye. The man is notably confused. He feigns a small wave and thoughtfully goes back to the album.

Band: **And the cat's in the cradle and the silver spoon,**
Little boy blue and the man in the moon.
"When you coming home Dad?" "I don't know when,
But we'll get together then,
You know we'll have a good time then."

I've long since retired, and my son's moved away.
I called him up just the other day.

The man picks up the phone with renewed excitement and dials animatedly speaking at first, then pauses. His face falls as he realizes that his son has no time for him.

Band: **I said, "I'd like to see you if you don't mind."**
He said, "I'd love to, Dad, if I can find the time.
You see, my new job's a hassle, and the kids got the flu,
But it's sure nice talkin' to you."

The man very slowly hangs up the phone, closes the album, and places it back on the table.

Band: **And as I hung up the phone, it occurred to me,**
He'd grown up just like me.
My boy was just like me.

The man remains seated and thoughtful, hands clasped, until song is finished. (Lower lights.) He exits.

Band: **And the cat's in the cradle and the silver spoon,**
Little boy blue and the man in the moon.
"When you coming home Dad?" "I don't know when,
But we'll get together then,
You know we'll have a good time then."

Words and music by Harry Chapin and Sandy Chapin.
Copyright © 1974 Story Songs, Ltd.
International Copyright Secured.
All Rights Reserved.

Transition and Prayer

Host

Our parents had great intentions, and we do too. We think that if we can grab some of tomorrow it will make today more meaningful. We need to slow down, stop, and look. Will you pray with me now?

God, all too often we so devotedly concern ourselves with our dreams, ideas, and plans for tomorrow that we forget to enjoy each moment as it comes. We confess that we have postponed the good life that you have planned for us. Forgive us, Lord. We so quickly neglect your calling.

Jesus, just as you took time to find a place to meet your Father, we take time now to see you, to feel your presence, to know your company. Thank you for new starts, for gentle attempts on your part to draw us to yourself, to the center of life itself. We give ourselves to you today, Lord. Amen.

Message

Speaker   "Stop, Look, and See"

Light sermon area.

Exit Music

Band   Director's Choice

Light band; show main graphic.

Celebration 2

Why, God?

Felt Need: To find God in the midst of pain and tragedy

Desired Outcome: To trust that God is ever-present with us, even in times of suffering

Theme: Why, God?

Word: Genesis 4:7–13

Metaphor/Image: A cross with blood on it, newspaper headlines, and a city skyline

The Lesson: Sometimes the tragedies of life overwhelm us. We see injury, abuse, hunger, disease, and violence, and we find ourselves asking "Where is God? Why would God let this happen?"

This celebration reminds us that ultimately God comes and joins us in our pain. Jesus bore our pain and sorrow—as well as our sin—on the cross.

The Look: We constructed a "living altar" display using a wooden cross, newspaper clippings, and red candles. We laid the cross diagonally on its side, and fastened headlines and pictures of violence and crime from the newspaper on the cross. Then we spattered the cross with red paint to represent Christ's blood. We surrounded the cross with tall candle stands containing red candles.

Worship Celebration

Play Kirk Franklin CD before service begins.

Video Clip

from *Shawshank Redemption*

Lower house lights; begin video on cue from floor. Show scene where Morgan Freeman talks about pain while sitting on the bleachers in the prison yard.

Opening Music with Video

Band   "Land of Confusion"

Light band; play video clips from The Century: America's Time with Peter Jennings *showing several acts of violence, including footage about the assassination attempts on Wallace and Reagan.*

Call to Worship

Host 1

Light speaker and project onscreen; project graphic on cue (*).
Have choir move to stage at the end.

You and I live in a land of confusion. Every day we hear about death and disease, tragedy and betrayal, poverty and pain. And all of us have at least once found ourselves asking, *Why do these things happen, God? Where are you in the midst of suffering?

Yet God is no stranger to pain. Jesus was born into discomfort and died in agony. And the Bible says that Jesus took on our grief, and carried our sins and sorrows as his own.

We gather today as people who have experienced the deep wounds of pain in our lives and asked *why*? We are hungry to hear the voice of hope, to know that God hears our cries. Our hope today is that God does hear and does join us in the depths of our pain.

Listen as the choir (band) calls us to worship.

Feature Song

Female Vocal, Band, and Choir   "Now Behold the Lamb"

Light band and choir.
End by having the host recite the paraphrase of Isaiah 53 while the band continues to play softly in the background.

From Isaiah 53:3-5:
>He was despised and rejected
>>a man of sorrows and familiar with suffering.
>
>Like someone we hide from.
>>He was despised and we gave him no respect.
>
>Surely he took on our pain
>>and carried our sorrows
>
>And it appeared as though even God had left him. Alone.
>
>But he was pierced for our sins
>>he was crushed for our failures
>
>The punishment that brought us peace
>>came down on him
>
>And by his wounds we are healed.

Song Celebration

Band   **"Nothing But the Blood of Jesus"**
                                  "What a Mighty God"

___

Project words; have leader ask audience to stand.

Responsive Prayer

Host 1   **from Psalm 72**

___

Light speaker; play soft music under.
Project words onscreen. Ask audience to be seated after reading.

We recognize and affirm our mighty God today. Will you join me as we share this prayer from Psalm 72 as a declaration of our alignment with the God who gave so much in order to identify with us. I will begin.

Leader: O God of love, give to your children the grace to represent you effectively in our discordant world, our land of confusion.

People: Give us the courage to put our lives on the line to communicate life and truth to all people wherever they may be found.

Leader: Where there is injustice…

People: May we discover its cause, and proclaim its cure.

Leader: Where there is bigotry…

People: Teach us how to love and how to call others to love.

Leader: Where there is poverty…

People: **Help us to share the wealth that has come from you.**

Leader: Where there is war and violence…

People: **Make us peacemakers that lead men and women to your peace.**

Leader: Help us, O God, to become what you have appointed and empowered us to become. Where there is darkness…

People: **May we become the rays of your sun that banish the gloom from lonely lives.**

Leader: Where there is drought…

People: **Let us be the gentle showers that turn barren deserts into green meadows.**

Leader: Where there is ugliness and distortion…

People: **Enable us to portray the beauty and grace of your way, your life. Amen.**

Adapted from Leslie Brandt, *Psalms/Now* © Concordia Publishing House, 1973, pp. 119–120. Used by permission.

Song of Response

Female Vocal, Band, Choir, and Congregation — **"Now Behold the Lamb"**

Resume song and project words.

Announcements

Host 2

Have choir exit.
Light speaker; project graphics.

Offering and Featured Music

Band — **"Even God Must Get the Blues"**

Light band and project onscreen.

Message

Speaker — **"Sprinkle This Blood"**

Light speaker and project with graphics on cue.

Send Out

Host 1
_____

As before; use key lines from Psalm 72 for the dismissal.

Exit Music

Band   **"Now, Behold the Lamb"**
or
"What A Mighty God"
_____

Project graphic; light band.

Celebration

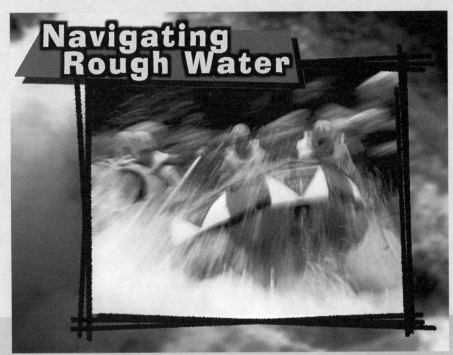

3 Navigating Rough Water

Felt Need:	To find comfort and encouragement during difficult times
Desired Outcome:	To recognize and experience God's sustaining presence
Theme:	Navigating Rough Water
Word:	Mark 4:35-41
Metaphor/Image:	White-water rafting
The Lesson:	Although we'd prefer smooth sailing on untroubled waters, sooner or later we will encounter rough and stormy waters. Experiences of illness, death, loss, and failure are a normal part of life, but by sharing painful experiences with one another, we can "comfort others with the same comfort we have received" (2 Cor. 1:3-4). The people of God must remind one another of God's goodness and sustaining love and be encouraged!
The Look:	Create a rafting-trip scene by using a a medium-sized raft with oars. If you can borrow several fake rocks (from a landscape or outdoor store) or make your own, add these to the scene for a more adventurous feel! Rather than candles, consider using a Coleman lantern, lit and perched on a rock. Be mindful of the local fire code, regarding propane, inside your structure.
Featured Option:	Communion

Worship Celebration

Play a CD of wind and ocean sounds or extended video footage of white-water rafting.

Opening Music with Video

Band   **"Running on Empty"**

Light band; project video footage of white-water rafting if available. (Check your local library.)

Call to Worship

Host

Light host; project host, then main graphic on cue (*).

In the boat of life, have you ever felt that all the big waves were coming straight at you? In a matter of moments, your world was turned upside down. You've suddenly gone from calm to chaos, from peace to perplexity.

The pink slip comes.
The doctor calls.
The divorce papers arrive.
The check bounces.
The policeman knocks on your door.

Your serene world turns stormy. You are hail-stormed by distractions, assailed by doubts, pummeled by demands. And you can't quite figure out how to get from sorrow to celebration. How do you find God amidst the chaos?

We come today to discover how to *navigate life's rough water, how to enjoy God's presence when the waters threaten to overwhelm us. Let us seek the God who holds us safe and steady in the midst of life's turbulence. Stand as we sing and worship together.

Song Celebration

Band   **"Seek First"**
"I Can't Stop Thinking About You"

Light band; project words for chorus of "I Can't Stop Thinking About You."

Video Clip   from *River Wild*

Lower house lights; immediately begin playing clip. Scene is from the end of the wild ride, where Meryl Streep and family are silently hurtling downstream.

Follow-Up and Prayer

Host

Light host and project onscreen.
Softly play "He Won't Let You Go" on piano during the prayer.

When I see that video clip I always think that if I were in that raft, I'd sure want some-body with me who knew what to do, how to steer the boat. Sometimes life gets pretty scary. Circumstances strike. Life gets out of our control. The good news is that Jesus is in the boat, and he's been through it all before. He knows the course.

You're under the gun at work? Jesus understands.
You've got more to do than seems humanly possible? Jesus cares.
Do people take more from you than they give? Jesus knows how you feel.
Your teenagers won't listen? Your students won't try? Your employees
    return blank stares when you assign tasks? Believe me, Jesus can relate.

Will you bow your heads with me now? Take a moment to reflect about where your rough waters are. What waves billow up and distract you from knowing God's pres-ence? As you identify your distractions, picture Jesus there with you in the middle of your chaos. Hear his words of promise:

When you pass through the rough waters, I will be there. You will not
    be overwhelmed.
I have already experienced it all—all the pain, all the testing—and can help.
I am with you always, even until the end of the world.
That's my parting gift to you—peace. I won't leave you feeling abandoned.
    So don't be upset; don't be distraught.

Thank you God that you do for us what we cannot do for ourselves. You allow us to experience all of life and promise to stick by us through it all. Teach us to seek you above all else. Amen.

Featured Music and Testimonies

2 or 3 Speakers   "He Won't Let You Go"

(Ask two or three persons to describe stormy times in their lives, and how God delivered them from their troubles.)

Light speakers and piano; project speakers.
After each testimony is finished, sing "He Won't Let You Go."

Welcome and Announcements

Host

Light host.

Offering and Songs of Faith

Band   **"Surely the Presence"**
"Oh Lord, You're Beautiful"

Light band; project words.
Have congregation remain seated during the singing.

Message

Speaker   **"Navigating Rough Water"**

Light speaker during sermon; possibly play video clip if it fits better here.

Closing Music

Band   **"He Won't Let You Go"**

Light band.
Repeat white-water footage, then freeze clip.

Sending Out

Host

Light host.
Continue projecting frozen video clip.

Most of life isn't lived in the midst of still waters. The good news is that the God who calmed the disciples' fears that stormy day is also present in your boat. Be encouraged and enjoy the ride in the days to come. Amen.

Exit Music

Band   **"Running on Empty"**
or
"He Won't Let You Go"

Light stage; project main graphic.

Celebration

Taking Your Life Off Pause

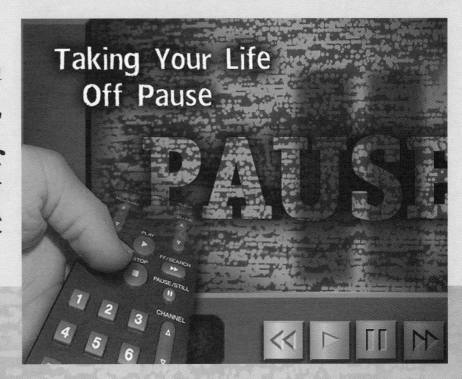

Taking Your Life Off Pause

Felt Need: Possibilization—To know that I have the potential to affect the lives of others

Desired Outcome: To leave with hope and the commitment to do the hard work of deep discipleship (during Lent)

Theme: Taking Your Life Off Pause

Word: Matthew 26:43-46

Metaphor/Image: Remote control and pause button

The Lesson: Strange how our lives can move so quickly from "can't complain" to "stuck in a rut." People of all ages experience that sense of being stuck when they do the same activities, day in and day out, like a remote controlled video "stuck on pause." To free ourselves from this inertia, we must be willing to respond to God's call, to stand up and walk into God's next plan. Like the lame man at the pool of Bethesda, we are called to stand up and walk.

The Look: To be consistent with the main graphic, place a wide variety of TVs and remotes on the stage. Having the TVs turned to a static channel is especially effective (make sure the sound is muted).

Featured Option: Communion

Worship Celebration

Have choir move in place before service begins. As choir moves up, begin instrumental. Light the choir once they are in place.

Opening Music

Choir and Lead Vocal   **"I Need You More"**

Light choir and band and project them onscreen during music; project words on cue for congregation participation.

Call to Worship

Host

Light host and project him or her during the Call to Worship. Then project main graphic on cue (*). Ask congregation to stand.

You know, there are words we use a lot in the 90's that I barely ever used in my childhood. Many are on this remote control. *Power, search, mute, pause* . . . Pause. That's what you need when you're in the middle of a movie and nature calls. Everybody knows that.

The trouble is, most of us have somehow pushed the pause button in life, and we don't even know it. We lack the power to get on with God's best plan.

We come today to be challenged to do the hard work of taking the next step. God calls us to get our lives *unstuck and off pause.

Let's stand now as we focus on God's presence and power.

Song Celebration

Band and Choir   **"Come, Now Is the Time"**
                                             "I Can't Stop Thinking About You"

Light choir and band; project words.

Announcements and Offering

Host

Light host; project host onscreen as well as graphics (as possible).

God calls us to be a generous community. Let's give our offerings now as the choir ministers in song.

Featured Music

Choir with Female Vocal Lead   "Still I Will Trust You"

Light choir and band and project them onscreen.
After song, choir exits.

Storytelling and Prayer

Female Player

Light player and project onscreen during storytelling. Have the storyteller stand center stage and not use any props. Begin soft music during prayer.

For a long time this story in John 5 didn't make sense to me. It seemed like it was about a loser—a whiner—stuck in his own predicament. But somehow he grabs Jesus' attention and becomes the recipient of a gift far beyond what he had ever hoped for.

Jesus encounters this man near a large pool of water north of the temple in Jerusalem. It's a huge, deep pool with five porches overlooking it. It's a monument of wealth and prosperity, but its residents are people of sickness and disease.

This story takes place in a town called Bethesda, but it could just as easily have been set in Central Park, Metropolitan Hospital, or even Joe's Bar and Grill. Those sick people lying by that pool could be the homeless huddled beneath a downtown overpass. This scene could take place anywhere there is a collection of hurting people.

Picture a battleground strewn with wounded bodies, and you see Bethesda. Imagine a nursing home overcrowded and understaffed, and you see the pool. Call to mind the orphans in Bangladesh or the abandoned in Sarajevo, and you will see what people saw when they passed Bethesda: an endless wave of groans, a field of faceless need. They came to the waters every single day hoping to be touched by a healing angel. The waiting had become their life.

When Jesus encounters this particular man, he is moved to ask the million-dollar question. But Jesus doesn't assume that everyone wants to walk, to be totally alive, so he poignantly probes:

"Do you want to be well?"

The man stammers and manages two rather lame excuses—pardon the pun. His condition had taught him to feel accused rather than loved. Whether Jesus was overcome with compassion or simply impatient for action, he gives this direction:

"Stand up. Pick up your mat and walk."

Against all conventional wisdom and the experience of 38 years, this man decided to give it a try. His gnarly legs struggled to push against the hard ground. His strong arms reached up and groped for security to stand vertically after a lifetime of being horizontal. Immediately he was well. He picked up his mat and began to walk. Small, hopeful steps.

Prayer   **"Do You Want to Be Well?"**

Spoken at the close of drama by storyteller.
Softly play song during prayer.

God, most of us are some way stuck in a horizontal mode. To stand up and walk will require a decision. When you say we're forgiven, we need to let go of our guilt. When you say we're valuable, we have to believe you despite how we feel. When you say we have eternal life, we need to bury our fear and get on with the living. When you say, "Stand up!" we need to do it.

Player exits.

Song Reprise

Band with Lead Vocal   **"I Need You More"**

Light band.
Project words, chorus only.

Message with Video Testimony

Speaker   **"Taking Your Life Off Pause"**

Light sermon area; play video clip (lower house lights); consider using video testimony of Carolyn Slaughter (available on Highlights '97 *video) about the healing of her marriage. Or tape a local video testimony.*

Communion

Host with Pastors Assisting

Light altar; classical guitarist plays in background; band in place at closing.

Sending Out

Speaker

Light speaker and project the speaker onscreen.

Exit Music

Band   **"I Can't Stop Thinking About You"**

Light band; project main graphic.

Celebration

5 Resurrected Hearts

Resurrected Hearts

Felt Need: Hope for our lives

Desired Outcome: To embrace a living relationship with Jesus

Theme: Resurrected Hearts

Word: Ephesians 3:16-20

Metaphor/Image: Open hands in front of light shining from the heart

The Lesson: There's no life in simply acknowledging the resurrection as a cerebral fact. True life in God becomes real only as we personally experience the resurrection of our hearts. The part of us that was dead comes to life with the breath of God as the life force. When we realize this as a gift available to all humankind, hope is born. The eternal God lives in us!

The Look: To replicate the glowing look of the cross in the main graphic, we used gobos (patterned templates) on the theater lights and shone them on dark curtains. Well-placed candle stands are always great for atmosphere.

Worship Celebration

Play jazz CD before service begins.
Have band move onstage before video begins.

Call to Worship with Opening Video Animation

Host

Lower house lights.
Light speaker; project video, "God in Me" from MSWII resource video along with script below:

In the beginning God created the heavens and the earth. God created the light and water, the plants and animals, but it was not enough. And so God created man in God's own image. God formed the man from the dust of the ground and breathed into his nostrils the breath of life, and the man became a living being. But it was not enough.

Though God's light streamed into all the world, men and women everywhere ran for the darkness. Like young children, they struggled to free themselves from God's parental care. But God still loved the world, so God sent his one and only Son, to show us real love. Anyone who believed in Jesus would have real life. . . . and that would be enough.

Of course, anyone who has not welcomed this invisible, but clearly present, God won't know what we're talking about. But if you welcome God, you will experience life on God's terms. You will be made truly alive—just as Jesus was raised from the dead. With God's Spirit living in you, your body will be as alive as Christ's!

We come this weekend celebration to embrace a living relationship with Jesus Christ. Let's stand and join together now to sing and enjoy the living God.

Song Celebration

Band
"Step by Step"
"I Could Sing of Your Love"

Light band; project words.
Leader prays briefly after "Step by Step."

Mission Moment

Host

This is a great opportunity to highlight a ministry in your congregation. Prepare a video about this ministry or have someone involved in the ministry tell about it.

If you have a video, lower house lights and play the clip.

Follow-Up and Offering

Host

Light speaker; project the speaker, then go to main graphic.
Host calls for ushers.

Featured Music

Band   **"The Long Run"**

Continue lower house lights.
Light the band and project them onscreen.

Message

Speaker   **"Resurrected Hearts"**

Light sermon area.

Prayer

Host and Band   **"I Need You More"**

Light speaker.
Have band softly play and sing during the prayer.
Project main graphic and then words to song.

Lord, our hearts are full of praise because you have set us free. Let us open ourselves to all you would have for us. We love you.

Sending Out

Host

Light speaker and project onscreen.

Exit Music

Band   **"The Long Run"**

Light band; project main graphic.

Celebration

6

Extravagant Love

Extravagant Love

Felt Need: To be loved unconditionally

Desired Outcome: To be dissatisfied with our own limited capacity to love, and to allow God to change our hearts and motives

Theme: Extravagant Love

Word: John 12:3-8; Mark 14:3-6

Metaphor/Image: Emptied cologne bottles

The Lesson: We stand in amazement at the depth of God's love for us and are called to love one another as God loves us. But God's love is a hard act to follow: how do we show that kind of selfless, sacrificial love for one another? By borrowing from the story of Mary's outpouring of expensive perfumed oil on Jesus' feet, this celebration challenges the congregation to more genuinely demonstrate the extravagant love of God to others.

The Look: Drape the altar or a table with fabric and place a variety of candles and bottles of perfume on it. To heighten the multisensory effect, you might want to spray a modest amount of cologne or other fragrance into the air of the worship space.

Opening Music

Band   **"What's Love Got to Do With It?"**

Lower house lights; light and project band.

Video, Part 1

On the Campus   **"What's it Mean to Love Someone?"**

Begin immediately; band can continue to softly play during video. Part 1 and 2 available on the MSWII media resource video.

Song Reprise

Band   **"What's Love Got to Do With It?"**

Light and project band.

Call to Worship

Host

Light host and project onscreen, then go to main graphic on cue (*).
Ask congregation to stand.

You woke up early enough to get a shower, down a quick cup of coffee, and throw the kids in the car. You made it to worship in fairly good time.

But what's love got to do with it?

You said a few brief hellos on your way in, found a seat, and scanned the bulletin for interesting bits of info.

But what's love got to do with it?

You'll sing a few songs, pray, and quietly listen to a message.

But what's love got to do with it?

While Jesus was visiting the home of a friend, a woman named Mary stood before him and emptied an entire bottle of extremely expensive perfumed oil onto his feet. This act was an ultimate expression of care and love. But those present were disgusted by her wastefulness. The perfume was worth a year's wages, which should have been given to the poor.

Jesus, however, understood: Mary had done something wonderfully significant, and *love had *everything* to do with it. We come today to be challenged to show that kind of selfless love. Stand with me now as we offer up our love to God.

Song Celebration

Band   **"Love You So Much"**
                                                    "Step by Step"
                                          "I Love You Lord" (a capella)

Light band; project words.

Video, Part 2

On The Campus   **"What Does it Mean to Love God?"**

Lower house lights; begin playing video immediately after song.

Reflective Prayer With Scripture

Host and Band

Light speaker and band; project main graphic.

We can love only because God first loved us. So our love is always a *response* to God's love. Even though we know that God loves us, we sometimes don't feel very loving or lovable. Will you bow your heads to reflect and pray with me now?

Lord, we want to open ourselves to the promise that you not only love the world, but also that you love each one of us down to the core of who we are. You created us, and feel affection and wonder, delight and appreciation, for each one. Remind us always that we are truly loved, so that everything we do may be a reflection of that love.

(Band, Vocalists, and Host will recite.)

Host: Hear now these words of God's love for us:

Vocalist 1: God loves us and sent Christ, who through his death and sacrifice, cleared away our sins and the damage they've done to our relationship with God and one another. (1 John 4:9-11)

Vocalist 2: Can anyone or anything drive a wedge between us and Christ's love? No way! We can't be separated from Christ's love by trouble, or hard times, or hatred, or hunger, or homelessness, or bullying threats, or backstabbing, or even by committing the worst sins listed in Scripture. None of this fazes us because Jesus loves us. (Romans 8:35-40)

Vocalist 3: Tell the world: God's love never quits!

Vocalist 4: God says, "I have loved you with an everlasting love; I have drawn you with loving-kindness" (Jeremiah 31:3).

Host: God is love. When we take up permanent residence in a life of love, we live in God and God lives in us. This way, love has run of the house. (1 John 4:16-17)

You are truly the God of extravagant love. Move in us to love others as you have first loved us. Amen.

(Adapted from The Message.)

Offering and Featured Music

Band   **"You Don't Count the Cost"**

Light band and project onscreen.

It's out of our love that we give to the One who loved us first. Will the ushers please come at this time?

Message

Speaker   **"Extravagant Love"**

Light sermon area; project graphics on cue.

Sending Out

Host

Light speaker; project main graphic.

What's love got to do with it? For Jesus, love always has *everything* to do with it. Go now and immerse yourself in a lifestyle of love. Amen.

Exit Music

Band   **"What's Love Got to Do With It?"**

Light band; project main graphic.

Celebration

7 Real Followers

Felt Need: To find meaning for our lives

Desired Outcome: To help us move beyond mere belief to radical discipleship

Theme: Real Followers

Word: Luke 9:23-24, Ezekiel 37, Luke 24:45-49

Metaphor/Image: A ladder and a cross

The Lesson: This celebration uses a very postmodern, non-linear method of presenting the concept of what it means to be real followers of Jesus. We used the mixed metaphor of a ladder, representing our self-serving striving towards accomplishment, and a cross, representing the radical lifestyle of sacrifice.

The Look: Prominently display a cross on one side of the stage and a very tall wooden stepladder on the other side. For extra effect, place a pile of "dry bones" (from a costume store) on the stage. Having the speaker actually walk over to the cross, pick up the dry bones, or even climb the ladder makes for a memorable and meaningful demonstration.

Worship Celebration

Call to Worship

Speaker   **"Wake Up Call"**

Light speaker and project onscreen.

Our celebration today uses two images: a ladder and a cross. The ladder represents an image of culture: we are taught to be ladder climbers. Society tells us that real life comes only with success and achievement. That's not to say that having goals or working to achieve them is wrong; many of our goals are good. But sometimes we get the motivation wrong: we look for life and happiness through material things. We ask God to help us get the things we want—a promotion, a new job, a new house. We bring Jesus along with us, hoping that he will help us fulfill our goals and our dreams.

Standing against this image of the ladder is the cross. Jesus tells us that to be real followers we must take up our cross, change our direction, and follow *his* lead. We'll only find real life, real success, and real happiness by losing our lives. We exchange our worldly goals and dreams for the goals of the kingdom. Jesus said, "Follow me."

What does being a real follower look like? Where are the real followers?

Featured Music

Band   **"Empty Hearts"**

Light and project band along with graphic loop. (Animation available on MSWII media resource video.)

Transition to Video

Video   **"The Good Life"**

Lights down; begin video immediately. Available on the MSWII video resource.

Storytelling

Male Player   **"Ezekiel 37"**

Light area and project the player onscreen.

One day Ezekiel the prophet was passing time in the desert when the Spirit of God led him to a valley of dry skeleton bones and asked, "What do you think, Ezekiel? Can these bones live?"

Ezekiel replied, "Can't say God. You tell me."

God said, "Ezekiel, here's the deal. *You* speak to the bones. Tell them I will breath on them and cover them with muscle, flesh, and skin. Tell them I will bring them to life, and then they'll know I am Lord. But Ezekiel, this isn't really about dry bones; it's about people who aren't really alive. The living dead.

Message

Speaker   **"Dry Bones"**

Use outline for script. For more detailed information, see Real Followers: Beyond Virtual Christianity *by Mike Slaughter (Nashville: Abingdon Press, 1999), pp. 172-183.*

A. Dry Bones:
They were reminders of how the people of God were once alive, but were now spiritually dead. How do our hopes and dreams die? Because they are ladder-climbing dreams, not the living hopes and dreams of God.

B. Prophesy to bones?
What looked like life was not really life. Something was missing.
Example of Hall of Presidents at Disney World—the robotic presidents are amazingly lifelike, but not real. They only mimic real life. They are missing the animating power of the Spirit of God.

C. Ladder climb:
We postpone real life when we put things on hold until we've achieved our ladder-climbing goals. Give an example of a decision made for *life*.

D. Life is in breath of God:
Real followers are Spirit led, not success driven. We need to be sailboats—not speedboats—who move where God's breath is blowing.

Prayer

Speaker

Continue lighting the speaker and project the speaker onscreen.
Softly play music during the prayer.

Song Celebration

Band   **"I Need You More"**

Light band; project words.

Litany Prayer

Host

Light speaker; project speaker and graphic with prayer response.
Softly play music during prayer.

As I speak the prayer of our hearts, please join me by responding, "Lord I've been a believer. Help me be a real follower."

We've come together as those who believe. But believing is only the first step in the journey of faith. We must also act.

Lord, I've been a believer. Help me to be a real follower.

God, you have created us and wired us not only for relationship, but also for discipleship. We are to become part of the great movement of the Kingdom.

Lord, I've been a believer. Help me to be a real follower.

Jesus looked straight into the eyes of ordinary men and women and said, "follow me." Not because he needed a following, but because he knew that for those who make the choice, real life will follow.

Lord, I've been a believer. Help me to be a real follower.

Spirit of God, move us to let go of our so-called lives, so that we might find true life in you. So that we might truly follow you.

Lord, I've been a believer. Help me to be a real follower.

Touch our lives today, Lord. Lift us out of our complacency and inaction. Put muscle and flesh back on our dry bones. Breathe life into us. Amen.

Song Celebration

Band   "Open the Eyes of My Heart"

Light band; project words.
Have choir come onstage.

Offering

Host

Light host and project onscreen.

Featured Music

Choir with Female Lead   "I Go to the Rock"

Light choir and band; project them onscreen.

Storytelling

Male Player   **"Luke 24"**

Light player and project him onscreen, as he retells Luke 24.

Sometime after the resurrection, Jesus appeared to his disciples, ate with them, and explained the plan:

"Now you've seen for yourselves my suffering, death, and resurrection. You're the witnesses! Soon I'll send you power from my Father. Wait here for the promise of God-Breathed Life!"

Sending Out

Speaker   **"God-Breathed Life"**

Choir exits immediately; light speaker. For more detailed information, see Real Followers: Beyond Virtual Christianity *by Mike Slaughter (Nashville: Abingdon Press, 1999), pp. 172-183.*

Life isn't about getting to the top of the ladder, about achieving success. True life is found only when you open your sails to the wind of God, and go where Jesus leads. Real followers are Spirit led, not success driven. Our busy and complicated lives give us plenty of excuses for not following. But over-commitment is really under-commitment in our relationship to God: we say yes to so many things that we forget that we are also deciding no to other things. We must learn that not everything opportunity is from God.

If you had only one year to live, what would you do? What things would be important? What would not be important? Using the One-Year Rule can be a great tool to help you discover and focus on the things that are really important.

We need to live out of passion. A recent *Wall Street Journal*–ABC poll reported that more than fifty percent of all Americans would change jobs if they had a chance. We need to find out not only what we want to do, but more importantly, what God wants us to do. What is God's purpose for your life? Many good things will come along, but you need to be able to discern those things that are from God. Ask yourself whether or not something would be God's priority, and say no to everything else. Also ask yourself whether it will further God's purpose. If it not, then leave that task to someone else.

Downsize. With God, sometimes less is more. Have you ever thought about how much maintenance your stuff requires? How much time, energy, and resources go into it? Time is a limited and precious commodity. How much of your time is spent paying off your debts? Should you consider doing things that will make your life simpler like acquiring less, giving things away that you don't need, or making a commitment to only pay cash?

So consider this the first day of rest of your life. What will you do with it? Whose ambition will you follow?

Exit Music

Band   **"Empty Hearts"**

Light band and project.

Celebration

Pentecost— In Your Dreams

8

Pentecost
In Your Dreams

Felt Need: To be jolted into faith-filled living

Desired Outcome: To know the power of naming and living our dreams

Theme: Pentecost—In Your Dreams

Word: Acts 2:17-18

Metaphor/Image: Nighttime clouds and moon

The Lesson: Pentecost is a powerful time to remind believers of the reality and significance of experiencing the presence of the Holy Spirit. Without the Holy Spirit, we are simply mortals, but with the indwelling of the Spirit, anything is possible. Forgotten dreams become rediscovered reality.

The drama "Dreamer's Anonymous" asks the question when it was that we stopped dreaming for our lives. Finally, the invitation to reaffirm our own baptism at the conclusion allows for an alternative to the standard altar call.

The Look: Set up stations in strategic places on the floor of the worship area for baptismal reaffirmation. If you have the ability to incorporate gobos (patterned textures that cover lights), use a cloud or star pattern on the back walls to enhance the main graphic.

Featured Option: Baptism and/or Reaffirmation of Baptism.

Pentecost Worship Celebration

Opening Music

Band   **"Sweet Dreams"**

Light band and project them onscreen.

Call to Worship With Video Animation

Host   **"Pentecost—In Your Dreams"**

Available on "The Visual Edge" (Group Publishing).
Lower house lights; begin night sound effects and video animation.
Return to the main graphic at end of the Call to Worship.

When was the last time you laid on your back and looked up at the nighttime sky? (*Pause.*) Most of us probably haven't done that since we were children. Remember just lying there, gazing at the stars, watching the clouds float past? Remember all the dreams you had? Remember believing that you could do and be anything?

But we grow up and reality hits. While young children dream about the stars and act out their dreams, adults learn to settle for the easy life.

The New Testament event called Pentecost was about believers receiving the gift of the Holy Spirit for the first time, about God invading their lives. Jesus told us that this power would enable us to do anything—only the sky would be the limit. You and I are empowered to dream God's dreams and live out God's purpose. Pentecost—In Your Dreams!

Let's stand now and sing in celebration.

Song Celebration

Band   **"Awesome God"**
"I Could Sing of Your Love"
"Shine on Us"

Light band; project words.

Prayer

Host

Light host and project onscreen.
Play "Shine on Us" softly during the prayer.

Will you bow your heads and pray with me now?

God, remind us what it means to dream and to act on those dreams. Some of us have succeeded in living out our dreams, while others have found failure and disappointment. But Lord, no matter what our past might have held, we want to trust you for what you can do in the future. Teach us to seek your dreams and your purpose. Shine on us.

Song Reprise

Band   **"Shine on Us"**

Light band; project words.

Offering and Featured Music

Band   **"Missing Persons"**

Light band; project band and main graphic intermittently.

Drama

Five Players   **"Dreamers Anonymous"**

Light the players and project them onscreen.

Miss Fredo, the facilitator, is a bit frumpy. She seems hard on the outside, but we later learn that she's soft underneath. She believes she is keeping the group of dreamers from getting hurt.

Jud is a regular in the group. He's the open, vulnerable, blue-collar type.

Delia is a bit ditzy, and tends to takes on the point of view of whoever is talking at the time.

Arnold is the new guy. He's goofy and definitely a dreamer.

(Bring lights up on drama wing when the four players are seated.)

Miss Fredo: *(shutting the door behind her and walking around a bit at first)* I'm so glad you could come this week to Dreamers Anonymous. As you all know, this group meets weekly to assist in the recovery process for those struggling to fight their way out of the bottomless pit of…dreaming. As you are well aware, dreaming about what we could be or what great and grandiose things we could do can be deadly.

Delia: *(interrupting)* Isn't it okay to dream once in awhile Miss Fredo? I always preferred to think of myself as a social dreamer.

Miss Fredo: No. If I've seen it once, I've seen it a thousand times. You start out small with little birthday-candle wishes, then move on to sharing the turkey wishbone with Gramps on Thanksgiving. Before you know it, you've decided to study art at some expensive college that costs your parents twenty grand a year. Jobs are scarce, and soon you become your parent's worst nightmare. It just goes downhill from there.

Delia: Sorry, Miss Fredo. I was just asking a question.

Miss Fredo: Now then, for some of you long-termers, this is familiar territory. But for Arnold here *(motioning to him)*, this is his first go at recovery. He hit bottom last week and…well, Arnold, why don't you tell us your story?

Arnold: OK, Miss Fredo. *(Stands to speak.)* Hello, my name is Arnold, Arnold Spankum.

All: Hello Arnold!

Arnold: And I'm a dreamer. *(All react.)* I don't think I'm really that different from any of you. I was a normal child. I would lie awake at night sometimes, staring out my bedroom window at the full moon and the bright starry sky. First I'd find the big dipper. That would get me excited, and then I would begin to wish…

Delia: What did you wish for Arnold? What did you see?

Arnold: I would see…me. Sometimes I'd dream about being a fireman. I'd put out blazing fires and rescue frightened children. Other times I'd dream about being a great basketball star who was tall and aggressive and able to drive through any defense to make a big dunk. *(shouts)* Two points! *(He makes a pretend shot and falls clumsily on the floor.)*

Jud: Foul! He was fouled!

All except Miss Fredo: *(Echoing with Jud)* Right! Yeah! OK!

Delia: *(Jumps up and assumes a cheerleading position)* I wanted to be a cheerleader once!

Jud: *(Interrupting Delia)* Be quiet and let Arnold talk. How's he supposed to talk if you keep interrupting?

Delia: Can we say touchy??

Miss Fredo: Okay, go on Arnold.

Arnold: Pretty soon it wasn't enough to look at the sky or dream about shooting baskets. A few weeks ago… *(He drops off talking and hangs his head in shame.)* A few weeks ago, I began thinking I could make people laugh. You know, stand up and do funny things like the people on television. Like Jerry Seinfeld.

Delia: Ohhhh. That's a big dream, Arnold. Bigger than being a cheerleader.

Jud: And you know it's impossible, right? Even if you actually begin to think it's possible, you know that eventually you'll have to come back to reality.

Arnold: Well…

Delia: I've been in your shoes, Arnold. Lucky for me there were loving, caring people all around who intervened and got me back to a more safe and sensible place. Teachers, friends, and, most of all, my parents. They taught me the words I now start each day with:

> If it's possibly not possible,
> It's probably not probable.
> Just do the predictable,
> And keep my world comfortable.

(All are stunned and touched. Arnold begins softly repeating the words to learn them.)

Jud: Arnold, you can't expect to lick this in a week. It's taken us all a long time to get this far, and we still slip up.

Miss Fredo: Why don't you tell us more, Jud? How was your week?

Jud: Well, I messed up bad. Somehow I got the idea I could try to get a better job. Actually, I want to draw. *(All gasp in amazement.)* Well, just kids' books or something. So I took a step and called the community college.

(All gasp and look at Miss Fredo for her reaction.)

> *(Jud bursts out)* I just want to get all the pictures I have in my head down on paper. I want my life to count for something. I want to believe I'm here for a reason!

Miss Fredo: Then what, Jud? What did you do next? How did you overcome?

Jud: You told us to call someone when we felt weak, so I called my brother Roger. Good old Roger! He reminded me that Mom lined the kitty litter pan with my grade school artwork. What was I thinking? I'm sorry. Sorry.

Miss Fredo: It's OK, Jud. Just don't keep putting yourself in the awkward position of going for your dreams. You're too…

Delia: Boring?

Arnold: Insignificant?

Delia: Stupid?

Miss Fredo: No, but thanks for the help.

All: No problem. That's what we're here for. Anytime.

Miss Fredo: No. You're too…vulnerable.

Arnold: Vulnerable. I was going to say that.

Miss Fredo: (*continuing*) Life is tough enough without giving it an excuse to kick you in the teeth.

(*All are quiet.*)

Arnold: (*Clutching his mouth*) Oooo, that would hurt.

Jud: I don't even have a good dental plan.

Delia: Were you a dreamer Miss Fredo?

Miss Fredo: What? Oh, uh, yes, I'm afraid I was…But no more. I've recovered now. No turning back for me. (*She is wistful and on the verge of tears.*) No, I know my limits. I know my limits.

(*All look sad.*)

Delia: Miss Fredo, could we end tonight's meeting by saying the Reality Prayer? I need a boost of truth.

Miss Fredo: Great idea! Everybody stand, pull out those DA cards, put your right hand over your heart, and read the prayer together.

All: God, grant me the reality to accept what I can't change. The courage to resist changing what I can, and the wisdom to keep me from trying in the first place. Amen.

(*Fade to black.*)

Message

Speaker   **"Pentecost—In Your Dreams"**

Light sermon area.

Commitment

Speaker gives invitation for persons to reaffirm their baptism

Light speaker and project onscreen.
Project the main graphic while each participant is anointed.

Have the helpers anoint those who come forward by dipping their finger in the water and making the sign of the cross on each person's forehead as affirmation and reminder of their baptism.

Exit Music

Band   "Shine on Us"

Light band; project main graphic.

Celebration

Right Here, Right Now: A Radical Commitment

Right Here, Right Now

Felt Need: Indecision keeps our lives stagnant and faithless.

Desired Outcome: To make a decision to follow Christ in disciplined, potentially risky ways

Theme: Right Here, Right Now: A Radical Commitment

Word: Acts 24; Luke 19

Metaphor/Image: A parachute jump

The Lesson: We struggled to come up with an image to communicate what it's like to take an immediate leap of faith. The idea of a parachute jump came up as the perfect way to illustrate the experience of making a decision or commitment that once made, couldn't be gone back on. On that hot July morning, I had no idea that by 3:30 in the afternoon, I'd find myself 13,000 feet up in the air preparing to jump out of a plane! Why not try this amazing method of storytelling the "Zaccheus Adventure" yourself? The words are all here. All you have to do is "Jump!"

The Look: For a truly out-of-the-box worship experience, borrow a parachute and jumpsuit for the stage set-up. Arrange the parachute across the platform and have the jumpsuit hanging from a hook.

Opening Music

Band   **"Right Here, Right Now"**

Light band and project them intermittently with the main graphic during the chorus.

Call to Worship

Host (could be the person who jumped)

Light speaker and project onscreen.

We make hundreds of decisions everyday. Some, like deciding what to have for dinner, are pretty trivial. But other decisions require real action and commitment, "right here, right now." And that kind of decision can have pretty serious consequences. Saying no could indicate failure, but saying yes is risky and costly and will take everything you have.

I found myself in such a place this week.

Video

"The Idea"

Lower house lights; begin video immediately. Available from The Visual Edge, *Group Publishing.*

Song Reprise

Band   **"Right Here, Right Now"**

Light band and project onscreen.

Call to Worship (Continued)

Host

Light host and project onscreen with graphic on cue(*).

Whether it's jumping out of a plane or making the decision to follow the true Christ, the situation calls for decisive action: it's now or never. We so often reduce our response to the call of Jesus to easy intellectual belief. We believe in the idea of Jesus, and in the idea of being disciples. But do we act on that commitment? The mandate of the real Jesus was clear, and always demanded immediate action:

> "Come, follow me."
> "Get up."
> "Come with me."
> "Come to me."
> Jesus said to Zaccheus on their first encounter, "Come down immediately.
> I must stay at your house today."

*Right here, right now. It's time to decide. Let's stand and sing together.

Song Celebration

Band   **"Every Move I Make"**
                                                  "Step by Step"

Light band; project words.

Real Talk

Host leads

Light speaker; project main graphic.

Most of us struggle with being decisive and making commitments. In fact, we are the kings and queens of postponement. If you don't believe me, try staring at the prospect of falling 13,000 feet and see what kinds of excuses you come up with:

> I'll do it when:
> > I have more time…
> > I'm not so tired…
> > I can afford it…
> > My schedule isn't so hectic …
> > I'm sure I won't get hurt …

What are some of the ways we postpone following Jesus? (*You might want to allow the audience to respond aloud.*) We put off committing ourselves out of fatigue, fear, and false notions. Let's pray together.

Prayer of Confession

Host

Continue to light and project the host.

Lord, you say follow me, and we tell you how busy we are. You call us to get up, and we complain about being so very tired. You challenge us to come; we tell you to wait. Teach us Lord, to hear your call and to make the decision to jump—an immediate, decisive response to follow you without reservation.

Prayer Song

Band   **"Send Your Rain"**

Light band; project words.

Transition

Host
___

Light speaker and project onscreen.

As part of our commitment to Jesus and to this faith community, let's give our offerings as true disciples. Will the ushers please come as the band plays?

Offering and Featured Music

Band   **"Where He Leads Me"**
___

Light band and project onscreen.

Video

"The Jump"
___

Lower house lights; begin playing video immediately. Use video footage of my jump available on The Visual Edge *from* Group Publishing.

Message

Speaker   **"Right Here, Right Now: A Radical Commitment"**
___

Light sermon area; project graphics on cue.

Sending Out

Host/All   **"A Postmodern Confession of Faith"**
___

Light speaker; project words on screen. Consider shortening the confession or alternating paragraphs between host and all.

"I am part of the Church of the Out-of-Control. I've given up my control to God. I've jumped off the fence; I've stepped over the line. I've pulled out all the stops; I'm holding nothing back. There's no turning back, looking around, slowing down, backing away, or shutting up. It's a life against the odds, outside the box, over the wall, "Thy Will Be Done . . ."

I'm done playing by the rules, whether its Robert's Rules of Order or Miss Manner's Rules of Etiquette or Martha Stewart's Rules of Living. . .or Merrill Lynch's Money-Minding/Bottom-Lining/Ladder-Climbing Rules of America's Most Wanted.
I am not here to please the dominant culture. . . .I live to please my Lord and Savior. My spiritual taste buds have graduated from fizz and froth to Fire and Ice. Don't give

me that old-time religion. Don't give me that new-time religion. Give me that all-time religion that is as hard as rock and as soft as snow.

I've stopped trying to make life work, and started trying to make life sing. I'm finished with secondhand sensations; third-rate dreams; . . . .I can't be bought by any personalities or perks, positions or prizes. I won't give up, though I will give in . . . to openness of mind, humbleness of heart, and generosity of spirit. When short-handed and hard-pressed, I will never again hang in there. I will stand in there; I will run in there; I will pray in there; I will sacrifice in there; I will endure in there—in fact, I will do everything in there but hang. My face is upward; my feet are forward; my eyes are focused; my way is cloudy; my knees are worn; my seat, uncreased; my heart, burdened; my spirit, light; my road, narrow; my mission, wide.

I won't be seduced by popularity, traduced by criticism, travestied by hypocrisy, or trivialized by mediocrity. I am organized religion's best friend and worst nightmare. I won't back down, slow down, shut down, or let down until I'm preached out, teached out, healed out, or hauled out of God's mission in the world entrusted to members of the Church of the Out-of-Control . . . to unbind the confined, whether they're the downtrodden or the upscale, the overlooked or the under-represented.

My fundamental identity is as a disciple of Jesus—but even more, as a disciple of Jesus who lives in Christ, who doesn't walk through history simply "in His steps," but seeks to travel more deeply in His Spirit. Until He comes again or calls me home, you can find me filling, not killing, time so that one day He will pick me out in the line-up of the ages as one of His own. And then . . . it will be worth it all . . . to hear these words, the most precious words I can ever hear: "Well done, thou good and faithful . . . Out-of-Control Disciple."

—Excerpted from Leonard Sweet, *A Cup of Coffee at the Soul Café* (Nashville: Broadman & Holman Publishers, 2000), pp. 168-70. Used by permission.

Exit Music

Band   **"Right Here, Right Now"**

Light band; project main graphic.

Celebration 10

Wake-Up

wake up

Felt Need:	Possibilization and purpose for our lives
Desired Outcome:	To wake-up from our slumber and to follow God's direction
Theme:	Wake-up
Word:	Jonah 1:6
Metaphor/Image:	Alarm clock and pillow
The Lesson:	We all know what it's like to struggle with sleepiness. But have you ever considered that you can also be spiritually "sleepy"? Just when we thought we had all the time in the world, we hear the Word of God calling us to "wake up from our sleep!" This worship celebration uses multiple ways to drive home the this point: a video depicting the daily trauma of getting out of bed; the old favorite song "I Wish We'd All Been Ready;" and a drama that's a take off on the classic "It's a Wonderful Life." Everyone will get the message of this "timely" experience!
The Look:	For the drama, set up a couch, table, lamp, alarm clock, and a TV (turned away from the audience). In another staged area, we also had a large display of about twenty-five alarm clocks, with a few ticking for effect.

Opening Sound Effects

Alarm clock

Begin sound effects on cue; project main graphic.

Opening Music

Band   **"Sleeping Giant"**

Light band and project them intermittently with main graphic.

Call to Worship

Host

Light speaker; bring house lights up.
Project host, then project main graphic on cue(*).

Even though we practice waking up everyday, it never seems to get any easier. The alarm goes off, but we're often so sleepy that we don't want to get up.

For some of us, life can actually be like one long nap. The alarm goes off from time to time, but our tendency is to roll over, pull the covers of security back over our heads, and fall back to sleep before the sun has a chance to shine in. Hear these words from God:

> *"Wake up from your sleep."
> "Climb out of your coffins."
> "Christ will show you the light."

Stand with us now as we sing and worship.

Song Celebration

Band   **"Arise, Shine"**
"Every Move I Make"

Light band; project words.

Transition

Host

Light speaker and project onscreen.
Band plays introduction to next song after Host speaks. Host moves to stool with lead vocalist.

Amen. You may be seated. God is good! We are talking about the challenge to wake up as individuals and as a church, but what does that mean? We don't talk much about the end times, but the Bible speaks of a time when we could wake up too late and wish we'd done things differently. Listen now as the band tells the story.

Featured Music and Monologue

Band   "I Wish We'd All Been Ready"

Light band; project soloist.
Continue lighting host on stool; project graphic; continue playing instrumental music underneath; speaker begins during interlude of "I Wish We'd All Been Ready."

Let's bow our heads and go to God in prayer:

> Lord, make us aware of the areas in our lives where we need to wake up. For some of us it's an issue in our personal life. A tired marriage or a worn-out career. For others it's a ministry opportunity that we continue to put off, waiting until we have more time and energy. Or perhaps for some there is a something in our lives that we need to confess, to deal with, so that we can open ourselves to your enlivening call. Father, we thank you that you call us to wake up and renew our lives today. We ask these things in the name of Christ, through whom we have already received new life, and through whom we have been given power to live transformed lives. Amen.

Transition

Host

Light host and project onscreen.
Host calls for ushers to come forward.

It's good to be together for worship. We celebrate the abundance of God now as the ushers come to receive our offerings.

What's the difference between an OK life and a really wonderful life? That's the struggle that George and Mary deal with in this make-believe saga.

Drama and Offering

Three Players (George, Mary, and Clarence)   "It's an OK Life"

Lower house lights and light area. Project players onscreen.
Use audio effects and brief video from "It's a Wonderful Life" in the drama.

(George and Mary are watching "It's a Wonderful Life." As the lights come up, we hear the familiar sounds of Jimmy Stewart and Lionel Barrymore. George breaks in...)

George: Aw, Mary...I've seen this movie 500 times. Can't we just go to bed?

Mary: *(sighs)* George, we are pathetic. It's 11:30 and here we sit. Watching the years go by, no different than we were last year at this time.

George: What do you mean "different"?

Mary: I don't know. I guess I just thought that my life would become meaning-ful someday. You know, significant.

George: What are you saying? That we live *insignificant* lives?

Mary: Look at the last year, George. Can you name one way that we have made an impact on someone's life? Did we do something that made a differ-ence? Did we ever once take a risk, sacrifice something for a greater cause? Is there any purpose to our lives?!

George: *(thinking about this)* Define "impact."

Mary: George, can you even tell me where we went on vacation last summer?

George: Sure, we went to... uh, it was......Oh, where was it we went?

Mary: *(Not angry, but sadly resigned to their plight)* Good night, George. *(Exits.)*

George: *(Numbly)* Goodnight. *(He suddenly remembers.)* Yes! Indiana! We went to Indiana! And she says we don't have any excitement. My life is plenty significant. Why, just last month I gave $10 to the Channel 16 telethon. And...*(realizing what Mary said is true)* and...

Mary *is* right. The only significant thing I've done all year is to help underwrite a stupid purple dinosaur. How did my life get like this? I had dreams once, too. I dreamed about doing something like teaching or social work, about doing something to make a difference.

I sit in church on Sundays, punch the clock during the week, and spend the rest of my time on my computer. Oh Lord, I'm stuck in a mundane life, and I don't know what to so about it. Please help me find meaning in this life. *(Clicks on the TV and lies down to watch.)* There! Now George Bailey had purpose to his life! Why can't my life be more like that? Why can't it be...*(He drifts off to sleep. On TV, we hear George crying for help in the movie.)*

George: *(Having a nightmare on the couch)* Help, help! I'm drowning; I'm drowning! *(Clarence pokes his head up from behind the couch. The TV has faded out. He pokes George to wake him.)*

(Clarence is a modern-day young man, a smart-alek type. He is wearing a white running suit, and a ball cap or earring.)

Clarence: Wake up George. You're living a nightmare.

George: Huh?! *(waking)* Oh, I'm sorry. I think I was having a bad dream or some-thing. I thought I was drowning.

Clarence: *(Says matter of factly)* You were drowning.

George: Huh? Yes, well it sure seemed like it. Wait a minute? Who are you? How'd you get in here?

Clarence: Name's Clarence. And you sent for me.

George: Sent here? Who sent you?

Clarence: (*Looks up*) Well, God.

George: God did??

Clarence: Just a minute ago, you asked God for help. And he sent me.

George: Then you're...you're an...

Clarence: That's right, an angel. Actually, *your* angel.

George: All right, I'm still dreaming, aren't I? Besides, angels have white hair and (*looking closer*) no earrings.

Clarence: Hey—it's a new day. (*reaches over and pinches George.*)

George: Huh? Look, either I'm off my rocker or.... But you do seem real. (*He suddenly realizes something.*) Well, if I'm not dreaming, and you're from heaven, then that means God is really up there—right? I mean you have seen God, haven't you?

Clarence: Well, it's hard not to see God if you know where to look.

George: Then it's all true: heaven, God, everything.

Clarence: (*Looking up at some unseen onlooker*) This may be tougher that I thought. (*To George*) Why were you praying earlier if you weren't sure?

George: Well, I don't know. I mean, of course I believed. But I just didn't *know*. I mean, I knew, but.... Look, what do you want?

Clarence: To help you, George. You were drowning and crying out for help.

George: I just fell asleep watching that corny movie.

Clarence: No, you were drowning all right. Drowning in a life of mediocrity. You really do live a mundane life, George.

George: Hey, wait a minute! First my wife, and now you. I happen to think that it's an OK life.

Clarence: Oh, "it's an OK life." Isn't that great? Well, why don't we just make that a title for this whole drama? We'll make a movie about it. "It's an OK Life!" It'll be a classic! People will be sure to watch it every holiday!

George: I didn't know they had sarcasm in heaven. Oh, I know what's going on here. It's just like the movie. You've come here to show me that my life is better than I thought, how terrible things would have been if I had never been born, right?

Clarence: *(Pauses)* No, I don't think so...

George: Sure you did. Just like the movie. Let's go.

Clarence: No, that wouldn't work...

George: *(Grabs Clarence by the lapels)* Come on, you did it for him! Do it for me! Why can't you do it for me?

Clarence: Because, George, since you were born, nothing's really changed.

George: *(Lets go of Clarence)* Do you always just float down here to depress people?

Clarence: George, God has given you amazing abilities. You have great opportunities to make a difference in this world.

George: He has? When?

Clarence: What about your new neighbors down in 28B? They don't know anyone in the area. They could sure use a friend. Maybe even a new church.

George: How am I supposed to know that? Am I supposed to just traipse down there?

Clarence: Then there was a chance for you to help out financially when the Conrads lost their house last year. Or how about when you got that offer to teach junior high, but you turned it down because the pay was low.

George: OK, hold it right there. This family is strapped. We've got more bills than we can keep up with. It wouldn't be responsible to not pay the people I owe. You can't lay all this pressure on me.

Clarence: I'm not here to pressure you, George. You asked for a life with more excitement and significance. I'm trying to show you what a difference you could make. George, you really could have a wonderful life.

George: I want to, Clarence. I really do. I always say I want to do the God thing. But when an interruption comes or when it's going to cost me something, I'd rather not be bothered. *(Clarence turns to leave because his job is done.)* Oh, Clarence, you're right. I want to change. I don't want to waste my life. I want to LIVE. I want to LIVE. I want to...

Mary: *(Has entered)* George, are you still up? Who are you talking to?

George: Mary? Is that you? Are you real, Mary?

Mary: Of course I am. George, you're shaking. (*An alarm clock goes off!*) Well, I'll be. I never set that alarm! Wonder why it went off at this time of night?

George: (*In a daze*) Because, Mary, (*turns to audience*)—it's time to wake up!

Message

Speaker   **"Wake Up"**

Light sermon area.

Video Transition

                                        "It's a Wonderful Life"

Lower house lights as speaker exits.
Begin video clip. Select the scene at the end where George exclaims "It's a Wonderful Life!"

Sending Out

Host

Light speaker and project onscreen.

Exit Music

Band   **"Sleeping Giant"**

Light band; project main graphic.

11 Desert Detours

Felt Need: Feelings of loneliness and isolation from God

Desired Outcome: To gain hope that will sustain us during the dry times

Theme: Desert Detours

Word: Exodus 13:17–22

Metaphor/Image: A sign in the sandy desert

The Lesson: This celebration reminds us of two powerful truths: we all have had and will have desert experiences, but God is present with us even there. Just as God led the people of Israel out of Egypt and through the desert to the Promised land, so God also travels before us and beside us through our own wilderness times. Ending the celebration with Communion serves as a powerful and concrete reminder of God's ever-present love and guidance, even in the midst of the desert.

The Look: Sand is what we most closely associate with the desert experience, so we dumped about 50 pounds on a plastic tarp in the stage area. We then planted tall stools and candle stands into the sand for the stage talk. The communion elements, in another space, were also placed in sand.

Featured Option: Communion

Worship Celebration

Play a selected CD before the beginning of the celebration.

Opening Music

Band   **"Hold On"**

Light band and project onscreen.

Call to Worship

Host

Light speaker and project onscreen, then project main graphic on cue(*).

In the summer of '62 I was 8 years old, and my family drove a 1960 red Chevrolet station wagon to California for a special assignment my Dad had that summer. All in all, it was a wonderful trip, except for the long stretch of hot, dry, barren, sandy desert we traveled through. Though I longed for cowboys and Indians to appear, all I remember seeing was the occasional tumbleweed blowing across our path. I began to think we were out there all alone, and that we'd *never* come to the end of the desert.

*Desert detours. You've been there, too. Walking through life, you suddenly find yourself in a dry, barren place. It can be painful and frightening and overwhelming. And that's definitely not what you had in mind when you started the trip.

But if your journey looks a little barren right now and you are feeling lost and confused, remember that you aren't alone. This experience could be a perfectly normal desert detour; you are never out of the reach of God's care.

Stand with us now as we celebrate this God with our songs of faith.

Song Celebration

Band and vocalist   **"I Walk by Faith"**
                                                 "Open the Eyes of My Heart"

Light band; project words.

Stage Talk

Host and 2 Speakers

Light drama area and project speakers.

Host: We want to see God every day, but what causes the "the eyes of our heart" to open? When is it that we run to God the most? When do we cry out to God for comfort? When do we pray the most?

Speaker 1: Desert times. We run to God when we're hurting the most, when we—or someone very close to us—is afflicted or overwhelmed or stressed. We cry out for help when the dry sand stretches out for miles before us, and the end is nowhere in sight. That's when we fall into God.

Speaker 2: C.S. Lewis was a well-known British writer and Oxford University professor who wrestled with the question of why we suffer in a book called *The Problem of Pain*. "Pain," he wrote, "is God's megaphone to rouse a deaf world." Lewis believed that God can and does work through our suffering, in the midst of the desert places.

Video Clip

Host introduces   from "Shadowlands"

Lower house lights; begin video on cue. Select the clip where C.S. Lewis (Anthony Hopkins) is giving a lecture and quotes the line, "Pain is God's megaphone to rouse a deaf world."

Though some theologies and preachers focus only on a gospel of happiness and success, real followers should not be surprised by pain. In fact, Jesus himself spent time in the desert. We will too.

Prayer

Host and 2 speakers

Speaker 2: Let's bow our heads together as we look inside our hearts. (*Music begins.*) The desert may be where you are right now. It may feel like you've taken a huge detour in your Jesus-journey, and you can't make sense of it at all. Maybe you have experienced a loss of some kind: the death of a loved one, a divorce from your spouse, the loss of a job, or just a lack of direction. Maybe you are feeling depressed, having problems at work, or experiencing difficulties in your relationships with your kids, or spouse, or parents.

Speaker 1: In the midst of these desert places, you want to know that God does not sit idly by to leave you to wander through these experiences alone. Be assured that God *is* with you, that God cares for you through the desert times, and that God can turn these detours into blessings.

Host: Take a moment now to invite the Spirit of God to work in your life. Identify your desert place and picture Jesus with you there. (*Pause.*)

Song of Response and Prayer

Band   "I Need You More"

Light band; project words.
Have the three persons remain onstage.

Speaker 1: God, you see us, you know us, you touch us. You became one of us. We open ourselves to see you, so that you may work in our lives.

Speaker 2: Thank you for the presence of your Spirit here today. We trust you because of the amazing love you showed for us in the life and death of your Son, Jesus Christ. Amen.

Announcements

Host

Seated on stool, if desired.

Offering and Featured Music

Band   **"Hope to Carry On"**

Light band and project onscreen.

Message

Speaker   **"Desert Detours"**

Light the sermon area.

Communion

Band   **"He Won't Let You Go"**

Host leads with pastors assisting. Project communion graphic or elements.

Sending Out

Host

Project graphic.

The desert offers powerful lessons to those who are willing to learn. As you go this week, trust that the Spirit is at work in your life. Amen.

Exit Music

Band   **"Hold On"**

Light band; project main graphic.

Celebration

12 Outrageous Love

outrageous love

Felt Need: I have feelings of unworthiness

Desired Outcome: To experience the totality of God's love and acceptance

Theme: Outrageous Love

Word: Luke 15:11–32

Metaphor/Image: A father embracing his son

The Lesson: The story of the prodigal son illustrates God's outrageous love for us. Like the wayward son who is joyfully welcomed home without question or condition by his father, we too are embraced by God's love without regard to what we deserve. We find this outrageous love perplexing and unnerving because it doesn't operate according to our ideas of what is fair and just: a person should get what he or she deserves. In response to such outrageous love, we can only shake our heads and say "thank you." Encountering God's heart of acceptance in a fresh way makes this celebration an experience that will change everyone from the inside out.

The Look: Candle stands and baptism stations created the look for this experience. The graphics and songs used in this celebration enhance the theme of God's outrageous love.

Featured Option: New members

Worship Celebration

Play a selected CD before celebration.

Opening Music

Band   **"Kind and Generous"**

Light band; project onscreen.

Call to Worship and Storytelling

Host   **"The Prodigal"**

Light host; project graphics if available.

Is your God kind and generous? Do you picture the God whom you serve as a parent who has always loved you deeply, even when you were far from home?

One of the greatest parables Jesus told involved a father and his son. The son takes a hard look at life and decides to go his own way, to do his own thing for awhile. He leaves home with his inheritance, and winds up blowing the whole pile on liquor and sex and fancy clothes. He finally reaches the point when he doesn't have two cents to rub together; he must either go to work or starve to death.

So to survive, he gets a job on a pig farm. But he quickly realizes that the pigs are getting a better deal than he is, and decides to go home. There is nothing great about his decision; no real sign that he is sorry for what he has done. He doesn't seem to recognize how irresponsible he has been or how he has broken his father's heart. In fact, there's no indication that he considers his father as anything more than a meal ticket. He decides to go home simply because he knows he can get three square meals a day there. And when you're almost starving, that's reason enough.

He sets out for home, and on the way rehearses the speech he hopes will soften the old man's heart to let him in: "Father, I have sinned against heaven and against you. I am no longer worthy to be called your son." He figures that this should work, if anything will! So he practices the speech over and over, trying to get the inflection right, trying to sound appropriately humble and repentant. But just about the time he thinks he has it down, his father spots him from the top of the hill and starts sprinting towards him like a maniac. Before the son has time to get a word out, his father throws his arms around him, and knocks him off his feet with the tears and incredulous laughter of his welcome.

Outrageous love. It's love that can't be earned, that isn't deserved. It's really too good to be true. Though you may have known God for a long time, you may not have experienced the depth of this outrageous love.

We come together to affirm that no matter who we are, God sprints towards us, arms stretched wide, ready to welcome us with outrageous love. Let's stand now and celebrate together.

Song Celebration

Band   **"Where Do I Go?"**
                                            "Sweet Mercies"

Light band; project words.

Prayer of Confession

Lower house lights; project response graphic.
Band softly plays "Come Just as You Are" in background.

Host

We simply are not accustomed to the brand of love our Creator offers. We often assume that a holy God would be more irritated, disappointed, or even furious with our imperfections and sins.

I invite you to a time of prayer with me. Let us open ourselves and allow the Spirit to minister to us. After I speak the words of our hearts, join me as we pray together the words on the screen.

Project words for response. Display main graphic when host is speaking.

We go to great lengths to find assurance that we are loved. Deep down, we don't believe that we are worthy of that love. But Jesus died for us.

All: Thank you God for loving me just as I am.

God, most of us feel like prodigal children who have soiled the family reputation. But when you catch a glimpse of us, your heart skips a beat. You see the divine original in each one of us.

All: Thank you God for loving me just as I am.

You look below the layer of grime and see children hungry for love. You see past all our mistakes and dare to call us your pride and joy.

All: Thank you God for loving me just as I am.

Just as I am, without one plea,
It was Your blood shed for me;
And now You call saying, "Come to me."
Oh Jesus, God, we come; we come.

All: Thank you God for loving me just as I am.

Song of Response

Band   **"Come Just as You Are"**

Light band; project words.

Membership

Host

Light speaker and altar; play soft music in background. Project new members onscreen.

As vocalist finishes the song "Come Just as You Are," host and pastors will approach the platform, and the new members will gather in a semi-circle around the platform. Continue playing soft music.

This special group of people has recently completed a three-month membership class. They've gained a wealth of knowledge, been challenged in their Christian journeys, and grown closer to our Savior.

Some of those in this group desire to reaffirm the vows of their baptism. Baptism functions as the public statement of a person's relationship with Jesus, a statement that they will no longer live for themselves, but will totally sell out to Jesus, choosing a lifestyle that reflects and demonstrates his love.

Listen to (*name*) sing this prayer as we rejoice because of these brothers and sisters.

New members are reaffirmed as song is sung. Host asks questions of group (soft music under):

You have completed the process of preparation! You have studied together, laughed together, and come to know one another. You have come to the understanding of membership at (*Name of church*). Now you are indicating your readiness to join at a deeper level.

By answering the following questions, you share the commitments you are making with the entire congregation.

> Have you accepted Jesus Christ as your personal Lord and Savior? (*Yes*)
>
> Do you believe in the Christian faith as contained in the Old and New Testaments? (*Yes*)
>
> Do you commit to be a faithful member of Christ's church and to live a lifestyle honoring God? (*Yes*)
>
> Will you uphold this church with your prayers, your presence, your tithes, and your participation in ministry? (*Yes*)

Let's pray together:

> Lord, thank you for these servants who have listened, learned, and taken this direction for their lives. May they be light in dark places, sold out to you and your kingdom. Amen.

(*Clapping*) Let's welcome these new members to our family.

Members return to their seats; host begins announcements.

Announcements

Host

Light host; project graphics.

Offering and Featured Music

Band   **"Amazing Grace"**

Light band; project onscreen.

Message

Speaker   **"Outrageous Love"**

Light sermon area.

Sending Out

Host

Light host and project onscreen.

Exit Music

Band   **"Kind and Generous"**

Light band; project main graphic onscreen.

Life: Live it Again for the First Time

13

Felt Need:	My life feels "stuck"
Desired Outcome:	To begin new lives in Christ
Theme:	Life: Live it Again for the First Time
Word:	John 3:1-21
Metaphor/Image:	Old TV's and video games
The Lesson:	A great seeker invitation, this celebration uses the video game "Pong" as a metaphor for everything that is old and stuck in our lives. Just as Jesus told Nicodemus he must "be born again," so we also need to get "unstuck" and have our lives reinvented in Christ.
The Look:	Old TV's, computers, and video games were arranged on the stage to create a nostalgic feel.

Worship Celebration

Have CD playing and project graphic before and between all celebrations.
Drama light and stage lighting effects continuous throughout.
Make sure house lights are down as much as possible (video intensive!)

Opening Music

Band, Female Vocalist, and Choir   "He'll Welcome Me"

Band begins prior to start time; have choir move to stage.
Light band only until choir is in place; project band and choir onscreen when vocals begin.

Call to Worship

Host   "Stuck at Pong"

Project ongoing animation of "Pong" video game.
Begin with animation; light speaker; go to graphic on cue (*).

Do you remember the video game, "Pong," from the mid-70's? We all played it and thought we had *really* arrived!

Now it's (*current year*) and needless to say, we've come a long, long way! Technology literally reinvents itself every day; it's continually changing. But what about us? Most of us are showing some signs of age and need a little reinvention ourselves.

Jesus said "You must be born again." We need to be reinvented, renewed, released. We need to *live our lives again for the very first time.

Today we affirm this message of hope. We come to worship and sing God's new song. Let's stand now and sing together.

Song Celebration

Band and Choir   "Heaven Is in My Heart"
"I Want to Thank You Lord"

Project words onscreen; light band and choir; choir exits following.

Transition to Top Ten

Host

We spoke a while ago about feeling a little old, but some of us aren't sure whether we're in the "old" category yet. So to help us out, we have tonight's Top Ten list from the home office in (*city and state*)!

Top Ten

Letterman-type Host

Use accompanying graphics and band sound effects.

Top Ten Ways You Can Tell You Might Be Getting Older:

10. While doing the hokey pokey, you put your right hip in and wind up in the hospital for replacement surgery.

9. You give up saying, "excuse me" when you pass gas because you can't hear it anyway.

8. You keep repeating yourself.

7. You find more hair growing in your ears and nose than on your head.

6. You send money to PBS.

5. You and your teeth spend the night in different rooms.

4. You keep repeating yourself.

3. You sing along to elevator music.

2. You hide your own Easter eggs.

1. One word—Rogaine!

Announcements

Host

Continue lighting host; use graphic enhancements.

Transition/Storytelling

Host   "Nicodemus"

Project host. If possible, play soft music in background before featured music.

The Bible is full of fascinating encounters that various individuals had with God. On one such occasion, a Jewish man named Nicodemus stole in at night to ask Jesus his most pressing questions. Nicodemus was a prominent leader who was very intelligent and religious, but he still hadn't found what he was looking for. When Jesus told him that he must be "born from above," Nicodemus was confused. He asked, "How can I be born again now that I am old?"

Jesus explained it to him. "This is about God's original creation of you, Nicodemus. I'm offering you a new beginning, a new life—*your* life. Live it again for the first time!" Nicodemus' question was a lot like the ones you and I have. Let's listen now as we give our offerings.

Offerings and Featured Music

Male Vocalist and Band   **"I Still Haven't Found
                                                                 What I'm Looking For"**

Light band and project onscreen.

Message

Speaker   **"Life: Live it Again for the First Time"**

Project with graphics; light sermon area.

Play video clip from Contact *at end as a response tool, to solicit action. Select video clip where Jodie Foster's character is sitting in the chair of the space capsule. Amidst many sound effects, she is fearful yet states, "I'm OK to go; I'm OK to go."*

Sending Out

Host

Continue lighting host; project main graphic onscreen.

Exit Music

Band   **"Heaven Is in My Heart"**

Light band; continue projecting main graphic.

Lay Down Your Gods

Felt Need:	To resolve the tension between our selfish desires and self-sacrificial love
Desired Outcome:	To help us recognize our false gods, particularly our materialism, and to respond to God's call to minister to the poor and oppressed.
Theme:	Lay Down Your Gods
Word:	Isaiah 58
Metaphor/Image:	Gold-covered, false gods
The Lesson:	Materialism can be a major distraction that keeps us feeling snug and comfortable. Yet Isaiah 58 reminds us that our riches are often at the expense of others. This celebration requires that we take a hard look at our lives, lay down our false gods, and make a decision to fully align ourselves with the mission of Jesus. This celebration culminates with communion, a reminder both of the meaning of true sacrifice and of the one true God.
The Look:	We collected a variety of items representing typical materialistic distractions—a TV, a set of earphones, a pair of shoes, a hubcap, jewelry, etc., and spray-painted everything gold. We set up a display of these items together with a pillar in their midst. At the top of the pillar we placed the bread and cup.
Featured Option:	Communion

Worship Celebration

Play CD and project main graphic before and between mains.
Special lighting on drama area.

Opening Music

Project graphic stills of people in need.

Band   **"Another Day in Paradise"**

Have readers stand as song finishes.

Reader's Theatre

Two Players   **from Isaiah 58**

Play soft music in background; light players.
(Have players bring stools up to stage); continue projecting stills.

Woman: And God said to Isaiah: "I need you to give this message to my people. Shout it loudly—don't hold back! They are turning away from me, and I need to get their attention."

Man: The people went to church, prayed at meals, and acted like they were eager to be called God's people.

Woman: "God, we've fasted," they said, "We've given up a lot. Why haven't you noticed?"

Man: But God said, "Even while fasting, you exploit your employees and your fasting ends in arguments. You strike at one another in selfish anger. Such behavior will not make me inclined to listen to your pleas."

Woman: Fasting is not for show or for giving a person the opportunity to brag about how spiritual he or she is.

Man: This is what God considers a fast: "Loose the chains of social injustice, and set the oppressed free."

Woman: God tells us: "Share your food with the hungry. Give shelter to the homeless. Provide clothes for those who need them. Don't turn away from others. You're *all* my creation."

Man: That's when God's light will really shine. That's when we'll be healed, too. Our integrity will go before us, and God will go behind us.

Woman: Then when we call, God will answer! We'll cry for help, and God will say, "Here I am."

Man: When we *spend* ourselves totally on behalf of the hungry and oppressed, that's when we'll begin to see the light. Our dark times will fade.

Woman: God will guide us and give us all we need on even the worst of days—even when everything around us looks dead.

Reprise

Band   **"Another Day in Paradise"**

as above

Call to Worship

Female Player

Light player again; project main graphic; player asks audience to stand.

Woman: Compared to so many in our world, we live in a virtual paradise. Our challenge is to identify with those who are hungry for food, for love, and for life. We need to lay down our false gods for the love of others. To lay down our lives for the One who laid his life down for us.

Stand with us now as we worship the Lord.

Song Celebration

Band   **"Crown Him With Many Crowns"**
                                                "You Alone"

Light band; project words onscreen.

Announcements

Host

Light speaker; project graphics onscreen.

Offerings and Featured Music

Band   **"Lay Down Your Gods"**

Light band and project onscreen.

Message

Speaker   **"Lay Down Your Gods"**

Light speaker. Project graphics on cue.

Responsive Prayer

Host

Continue lighting speaker while projecting response lines on cue; soft music under. Pastor breaks bread during prayer.

    All: **Forgive us, Lord, for ignoring your call.**
                Help us spend our lives for your sake.

    Host: Our Father who lives in the heavens,
                We want to honor your name.
                For your Kingdom to come, for your way to be done
                On earth as it is in heaven.

    All: **Forgive us, Lord, for ignoring your call.**
                Help us spend our lives for your sake.

    Host: Give us today only the bread that we need.
                Forgive us for our mistakes,
                And let us forgive others because we have been forgiven.
                Cause us to lay down the gods that enslave us,
                And thus deliver us from evil.

    All: **Forgive us, Lord, for ignoring your call.**
                Help us spend our lives for your sake.

    Host: For to you, Lord, belongs the Kingdom!
                The power of your Resurrection
                And the glory of reclaimed lives forever.

    All: **Help us spend ourselves fully for your sake. Amen.**

Communion

Pastor 2 and Band   **"We Fall Down"**

Light band and altar area if possible. Have band softly play "We Fall Down." Project main graphic.

(Holding up the bread and cup) We lay down our lives for the love of the One who laid down his life and his blood for us. Let us share now the life broken for us.

Sending Out

Speaker

Light speaker; project onscreen.

Exit Music

Band   **"You Alone"**

Lighting as before; main graphic onscreen.

15
God's Diary

GOD'S DIARY

Felt Need: To discover words and messages that can bring us real life

Desired Outcome: To integrate God's Word into our lives

Theme: God's Diary

Word: Psalm 119:32

Metaphor/Image: Indiana Jones paraphernalia and a diary

The Lesson: Postmodern people are not naturally enthused about reading an ancient book. But what if we identified that book as a treasure, as the very diary of God? This celebration captures all the mystery and adventure of one of our all-time favorite movies, *Indiana Jones and the Last Crusade*, and transfers it to an appreciation for the ultimate, ancient diary: God's true Word.

The Look: We created a display from old crates; leather boots, hat, and vest; an antique lantern; a rolled-up map; a rope; an old, rolled-up tent; a canteen; and most importantly, a large antique Bible. This display, together with the CD theme music, created a real atmosphere of adventure. We even had the speaker and host wear khaki shirts and jeans.

Worship Celebration

Play theme from one of the Indiana Jones' *soundtracks, before and between all celebrations. Special lighting on drama display throughout.*

Opening Music

CD   **Theme from *Indiana Jones***

Continue projecting main graphic; lower house lights.
Have band (and choir) come up at the beginning of the celebration (no lights).

Video

From *Indiana Jones and the Last Crusade*

Begin video immediately following song; keep house lights low. Select video clips from "Indiana Jones and the Last Crusade." The father (Sean Connery) and Indiana (Harrison Ford) are looking at the diary, which they found. This dialogue occurs:

> *Father: the breath of God, the word of God, the path of God. . . .*
> *Indiana: What does that mean?*
> *Father: I don't know, but we'll find out.*

Call to Worship

Host   **"The Diary"**

Light host; project main graphic on cue (*); begin percussion on cue (**).

As we gather for worship today, you and I have something in common with Indiana Jones. We have mail. *(Host begins to open a Bible wrapped in brown paper and tied with string.)* It's a message straight from the heart of God. But for some of us it's yet to be unwrapped—until now. The Bible is *God's Diary entrusted to us. (**percussion) It contains all the clues and discoveries that we need. And it provides a record of the God who has acted in history and who desires to be in relationship with humans.

Let's stand together and celebrate the God who wants to be found.

Song Celebration

Band/Medley   **"What a Friend"**
"Heaven Is in My Heart"
"Amazing Grace"

Light band and choir; project words onscreen.

Interviews in the Aisle

Host   **"Why We Don't Look in the Book"**

Light host; use cordless microphones on floor; try to have some prepared responses.

Today we have an opportunity to reflect on our habits. Most of us have been told that we should be reading our Bible on a regular basis. But I talk to a lot of people who find it really tough to make time for this discipline or to understand what they read. (Not anyone here, of course!) Why is it so tough? What are some of the things that keep us from the habit of reading?

(Host keeps it going from platform while a couple of people help field responses from the floor.)

Responsive Prayer

Host   **from Psalm 119**

Light choir or band softly; continue lighting speaker.
Begin soft music; project prayer onscreen, then return to graphic.

As a prayer together, let's say the words on the screen from Psalm 119:33-38.

> God, teach me lessons for living
>   so I can stay the course.
> Give me insight so I can do what you tell me—
>   my whole life one long, obedient response.
> Guide me down the road of your commandments;
>   I love traveling this freeway!
> Give me a bent for your words of wisdom,
>   and not for piling up loot.
> Divert my eyes from toys and trinkets,
>   invigorate me on the pilgrim way.
> Affirm your promises to me—
>   promises made to all who fear you.

(From the *The Message*, p.709-710.)

(Host finishes prayer alone.)

God, what a gift the Bible is! It contains all the treasure of you in one volume. Lord, shine down on us this day and rekindle our love not just for you, but also for your Word. Amen.

Prayer Song

Band   **"Shine on Us"**

Light band; project words to song.

Choir with 2 vocals   **"Order My Steps"**

Light choir or band; project graphic or musicians onscreen.

Announcements and Offerings

Host

Choir exits; light host.
Project graphics onscreen.

Featured Music

Band   **"Time After Time"**

Light band and project onscreen.

Message

Speaker   **"God's Diary"**

Light speaker; lower house lights throughout; play video clips on cue.

Clip 2: Scene where Indiana says, "May he who illuminated this book illuminate me."
Clip 3: The scene where Indy steps out to cross the canyon and a footbridge mysteriously appears.

Play theme CD afterwards.

Sending Out

Host

Light host. (Optional) Play theme music softly in background; project main graphic.

May God illuminate our hearts and our minds with the Word. Go this week and rediscover God's Diary.

Exit Music

Band   **"Time After Time"**
or
Theme CD

Light band; project main graphic.

16 The New Revolution

PRIESTHOOD
THE NEW REVOLUTION

Felt Need:	A feeling of staleness and untapped potential in our lives
Desired Outcome:	For everyday people to respond and join the Jesus Revolution
Theme:	The New Revolution
Word:	Ephesians 4:11–13
Metaphor/Image:	Hippie symbols including cross and "one way" patch on an army jacket
The Lesson:	Baby Boomers grew up in a world of "causes." Some say that causes are a missing element of postmodern culture. Or could it be that we simply don't want to be bothered?
	This celebration suggests that for Jesus people, there's *always* a revolution. God wants to take lives that lack real meaning and give them a cause and a purpose, to "reach the lost and set the oppressed free."
The Look:	We gathered '60's style props for the main graphic like an old army jacket and a variety of patches. For the drama set, we used a park bench, a guitar, and dressed the male player in a fringed leather vest and bandana. While this theme may seem a little "far out," we've found that a totally different look helps eliminate the "been there done that" feeling in weekly worship.

Worship Celebration

Play Larry Norman CD or other '60s music; project main graphic.
Pre-celebration lighting; keep stage lighting as low as feasible.

Opening Music

Band   **"Revolution"**

Lower house lights and light band; have choir move to stage.

Call to Worship

Host

Light host and project onscreen; project graphic.

"You say you want a revolution,
You know we all want to change the world."

When we were young, we had a lot of ideas about what we could do to change the world. But the days slip into years, and we begin to settle for the status quo. Before we know it, we've left the revolution to someone else: someone more qualified, someone more educated, someone with training and credentials like an ordained clergy person.

But Jesus gave us *all* authority to go, to teach, to serve and to make disciples. You don't need a title or a seminary degree. Jesus empowered us to be his revolutionaries.

When all of us get really serious about living out our faith, it *will* be revolutionary. Let's make a statement here as we stand and sing what we believe.

Song Celebration

Band   **"Can't Nobody"**
"Soon and Very Soon"
"Precious Lord"

Light band and singers; project words.

Prayer

Host

Project graphic; play soft music under; transitions to next song.

Lord, no one here wants to stand back in apathy. We all want to be part of a movement—*your* movement. Your Word says that we have authority to go, teach, give, and serve; but so often we think we can't. We think it means someone else: someone more educated, more qualified, more experienced.

But you persist in calling us to be your ministers, your servants, your revolutionaries. We are part of your plan to bring your love and light into this world. Show us a glimpse of what could happen if only we acted on your Word. What if, Lord?

Listen now as the ushers come to receive our offerings.

Offerings and Featured Song

Band and Female Vocalist   **"What If"**

Continue with lighting as before; project band and vocalist onscreen.

Drama

3 Players   **"Remember the Sixties . . ."**

After offerings are taken, light drama area.

It's the sixties. Two hippie-types are seated on a park bench playing the guitar and singing "Revolution." Their dialog is slightly "strung out" and exaggerated. Sunshine is slightly ditzy.

Bring lights up on drama area.

Both: "You say you want a revolution, well you know, we all want to change the world. You say that it's evolution, well you know, we all want to change the world."

Julius: Groovy man! I love the revolution . . . can you dig it, Sunshine?

Sunshine: Yeah, like, WOW man! This is a whole new level of existence in the universities!!!

Julius: Totally! I can identify, man. Only you mean *universe*, not *universities*. We're FOR the universe, but against all organized education and institutionalized government.

Sunshine: Like, Big Brother is watching!

A second girl, Empathy, enters carrying a picket sign that says "Free the Planet, Forget the Spray." She is saying goodbye to her friends from a distance.

Empathy: Peace, man! Love! Catch you later! All right! (*She comes in and sits down, exhausted.*) I am so strung out, man!

Julius: Just relax, baby, relax. Chill out!

Empathy: Well, I could tell you about my day. It was a happenin' thing . . . in the groove.

Others: What? Lay it on us, man. . . . (*Ad lib protests.*)

Empathy: Well, we all marched to the courthouse and stood for the cause. Crimson and Clover got arrested. (*Crimson and Clover sing. Sunshine continues singing over and over.*)

Julius and Empathy: (*interrupting*) Chill, Sunshine.

Empathy: It was the most mind-blowing experience I've ever had. It's like I'm part of something really big and expansive. I mean, if we don't set the world straight right now about aerosol cans and their deadly poisons, we'll never be able to save the earth. "Free the Planet, Forget the Spray!"

Others: Far out! Yeah!

Julius: I am definitely co-existing on that existential planet with you. Did you ever think we'd be doing this? One day we're sitting around being good little boys and girls, eating our lima beans in the school cafeteria, and the next thing you know we're leading the world in a revolution of peace, love, and harmony.

Sunshine: What is the cause, Julius?

Empathy: Sunshine, sometimes you are so way out there. You really need to reconnect. There's a revolution going on here!

Julius: It's OK, Empathy. Sunshine just hasn't heard the call yet.

Sunshine: The call? Hey, I'm trying just like everybody else, aren't I?

Julius: We're not talking about the rotary phone here.

Empathy: Sunshine, you are so unreal. You just sit here while the courts free killers on technicalities, and the government spends billions of dollars to send space capsules into the stratosphere. But you say you are "trying"? Why don't you get out there and picket like the rest of us?

Julius: Empathy, simmer down! Remember, we're about peace and love!

Sunshine: I just don't think I could really change anything myself. I'm just one person, after all.

Empathy: Sunshine! What about the *issues?* Do you want to wake up someday and find you have no water because the establishment says people should take showers every day?

Sunshine: Ban the showers, man.

Julius: Ban the soap! Yeah! Do you want your children's minds to be controlled by newspaper comic strips like Beetle Bailey and Family Circus?

Sunshine: Of course not. I just need a cause that's . . . me. Something that I can be part of . . .

(Speaker interrupts from the platform. Bring lights up on the speaker.)

Speaker: Hey y'all! I could tell you about a real Revolution. *(Have speaker ad lib.)*

All three players begin to make excuses to leave (ad lib), and get up to exit. Lights fade on the drama area.

Speaker turns to audience and decides to speak to them instead, telling them about the Jesus Revolution.

Message

Speaker   **"A New Revolution"**

Light sermon area; project graphics.

Featured Song

Band and Female Vocalist   **"In Return"**

Light band and project onscreen.

Sending Out

Speaker

Light speaker; project main graphic.

Exit Music

Band   **"Soon and Very Soon"**

as before

Celebration

17

Militant Love

Felt Need: To understand the true nature of love and how to handle conflict

Desired Outcome: To learn to love actively rather than passively

Theme: Militant Love

Word: Matthew 5:43–46

Metaphor/Image: Images of protesters inside the image of a cross

The Lesson: We use the phrase *militant love* because the force of Jesus-love must be stronger than the forces that would come against it, such as violence, envy, and hatred. The celebration confronts the parts of us that we would be more comfortable ignoring: learning to love the person who's lovability escapes us.

The Look: Combine the use of multiple candle stands with a large wooden cross laid on its side.

Worship Celebration

Softly light the cross and use pre-celebration lighting; project main graphic between all celebrations. Play designated CD prior to celebration.

Protest Video and Opening Music

Band   "I Want to Know What Love Is"

Light band; lower house lights. Consider using video footage of the civil rights movement. You must acquire this yourself.

Call to Worship

1 Male, 1 Female Speaker

Light speakers and project onscreen, then project graphic.

Speaker 1: The realities of life have taught us what love is *not*. We all need a strategy for confronting conflict, for learning to love across racial and cultural lines as well as across the kitchen table.

Speaker 2: Jesus knew what love was and often spoke of it, always addressing the topic as though his followers never quite got it. And though we have the supreme example of Jesus' love on the cross, most of *us* still don't get it. We claim to be proficient at love, but we often struggle to be agents of the grace that Jesus embodied.

Speaker 1: This celebration is about love—militant love. This radical love is not just a great idea a civil rights leader once had, but a strategy for daily living. That's our challenge. Let's stand together to sing and acknowledge our God who is love.

Song Celebration

Band   "Sweet Mercies"
"Every Move I Make"
"What a Mighty God"

Project words; light band.

Reader's Theatre and Prayer

1 Male, 1 Female Player

Light players; project graphics on cue, then main graphic for prayer.
Play soft music under.

Player 2: The striking fact that makes the words of Jesus Christ so powerful is that he lived those words to the extreme: Christ died for us. Militant love. Hear these words of Jesus.

Player 1: You've heard with the old written law, "Love your friends" and it's unwritten companion, "Hate your enemy." I'm challenging that. I'm telling you to love your enemies. Let them bring out the best in you, not the worst. When someone gives you a hard time, respond with the energies of prayer, for then you are working out of your true selves, your God-created selves. This is what God does. (Matthew 5:43–45 from *The Message*, p.21)

Player 2: Here's another saying that deserves a second look: "Eye for eye, tooth for tooth." Is that going to get us anywhere? Here's what I propose: "Don't hit back at all." If someone strikes you, stand there and take it. If someone drags you into court and sues for the shirt off your back, gift-wrap your best coat and make a present of it. And if someone takes unfair advantage of you, use the occasion to practice the servant life. No more tit-for-tat stuff. Live generously. (Matthew 5:38–42 from *The Message,* p.21)

Player 1: Greater love has no one than this, that he lay down his life for his friends. (John 15:13, *NIV*)

Player 1: Let's pray together:

As we pause to be honest with God, let me ask, who is your enemy? Who in your life seems impossible to love? Certainly we can all identify one person: a family member who has always underestimated you, a co-worker who seems to be only self-serving, a spouse that frustrates or annoys you. As you identify your enemy, silently admit to God your struggle to love that person.

Player 2: Lord, we want to be partners with you in reconciliation, to love others in our homes, our schools, our workplaces, our communities, our world. Show us first what really hides in our hearts—our pride, our shame, our judgment. Change our hearts, God. Shine your love into our hearts. Show us the meaning of your militant love. Amen.

Song of Response

Band   "Shine on Us"

Project words onscreen.

Announcements

Host

Light speaker; project graphics on cue.

Offerings and Featured Music

Band   "Spread Love"

Light band; follow vocalists with camera while projecting onscreen.

Message

Speaker   "Militant Love"

Light speaker; project graphics.

Exit Music

Band   "Spread Love"

as before

Celebration

18

Every Move You Make

EVERY MOVE YOU MAKE

Felt Need: To be able to choose my own future

Desired Outcome: To recognize the importance of our choices and to choose godly words and actions

Theme: Every Move You Make

Word: Hebrews 11

Metaphor/Image: The Game of Life™

The Lesson: We tend to think that we have relatively little control over our future: the future just happens. This celebration challenges that concept, and suggests that we do create our futures by our very thoughts, words, and deeds. That we can have an effect on our futures is a message of health and empowerment to all who dare to live purposeful lives in Christ.

The Look: Whenever it's possible to use a metaphor/image as well known as The Game of Life,™ the results are powerful. People already have a childhood familiarity with the image, which results in a more ready reception of the message. Our graphic used the colors and fonts of the game lid, and we created a display of the game set up on a table.

Featured Option: Communion

Worship Celebration

Play the designated CD; project graphic and continue the pre-celebration lighting.

Opening Music

Band   **"Every Breath You Take"**

Light band and project onscreen.

Call to Worship

Host   **"The Game of Life"**

Light host; project graphic on cue (*).

Do you remember "The Game of Life"? Remember the names of the spaces: Start Career, Start College, Get Married, Pay Day (never enough of those!), Buy A House? With every move you make, you get one step closer to retiring as a millionaire. It can be fun to play and pretend to live the life you always wanted, even for just a couple of hours. If only real life could be so simple.

You and I tend to think our futures are pretty much already mapped out. We believe there's really not a lot we can do to ensure what's going to happen. But Jesus knew something very powerful about life: Every thought he had, every word he spoke, every move he made had a major impact on the future. We're about to discover that the power of our thoughts, words, and actions can be an amazing force for accomplishing God's purpose in our lives.

*Every move we make matters! Let's stand and worship our God together.

Song Celebration

Band   **"Every Move I Make"**
                                                              "Almighty"

Light band; project words.

Mission Moment Video

Host introduces

Begin video on cue; lower house lights. Tape an example of a mission team at work, or tape the reflections of a member of a mission team.

Announcements

Host

Light host; project graphics.

Offerings and Drama

4 players (2 couples)

"The Game of Life"
David Hansen & Kim Miller

Note: This drama is longer than most. Move through the lines very quickly to get full impact.

The Players:
John—college student
Tracey—college student
Kyle—young professional
Kris—young professional

The Story:
Four friends gather one Saturday night to play a board game, "The Game of Life." Drama takes place in the living room of one of the players. A card table, 4 chairs, the game itself and some refreshments make up the set.

Drama opens as Tracey ENTERS with the game and a bowl of chips. She begins setting up the game, unfolding the gameboard, sorting out the fake money, etc. As she works, she talks loudly to John who is OFFSTAGE.

Tracey: John?

John: *(offstage)* Yeah?

Tracey: Could you see if there's enough ice in the freezer? I forgot. I might not have enough.

John: *(offstage)* Sure.

(There is a short silence. Tracey stops her business, waits, and frowns.)

Tracey: Well?

John: *(offstage)* Well, what?

Tracey: Is there enough ice or not?

John: *(offstage)* Well, it depends.

(Tracey sighs.)

Tracey: *(impatient)* John…

(John ENTERS casually; he has a smirk on his face. He holds a glass of Coke.)

John: Because if you were planning to do some cryogenic freezing or something, you might want to run down to Kroger.

(She glowers at him.)

Tracey: Four drinks for Kris, Kyle, you, and me. You do remember that your brother is coming over, don't you?

(John notices Tracey setting up the game and frowns.)

John: Oh man! I though we were going out.

Tracey: We can…later. I thought it would be fun to just hang out first. We'll just play a short game.

(She holds up the game box for John to see.)

Tracey: Tah-daa!

John: Life!

(He puts down his drink and grabs the box.)

John: Oh wow, cool! Life! Did you know I haven't ever played this game?

(Tracey grimaces. John looks at the game board on the table, then at Tracey.)

John: A short game? C'mom Trace, we'll be here for days.

(He traces his finger over the board and reads aloud a square where there is a high cash reward. Just then Kyle and Kris ENTER with their own snacks, engaged in conversation. John holds up the game box.)

John: Tah-daa!

(Kris and Kyle are excited when they see it.)

Kris: I love Life! This is like my favorite game! I love those little cars with the little people in 'em.

Kyle: *(very unexcited)* Wow, I'm thrilled!

Tracey: Yeah!

Kyle: I know it will be tough on the insurance, but I'll take the red car.

(Tracey is still sorting the money.)

Tracey: I think we're just about ready to start.

John: *(to Kyle)* So, did *you* agree to this?

Kyle: To what?

John: To play a board game?

Kyle: No, just to being *bored*.

Tracey: Oh, you guys! It'll be fun.

John: Hey, I didn't say it wasn't going to be. Actually, I like the idea of having a little control over my future for a change.

Kris: Sounds like a personal problem to me.

Kyle: Very personal. In fact, please don't share!

(Light laughter.)

(Tracey rolls her eyes. They all sit. There is excitement as each one picks their little cars, and the money is stacked up. They make various jokes about the fake money. Everyone is getting into it, laughing, reading some squares, etc. After a few minutes, they put their pieces at the start and are ready to go.)

Kris: All right, who goes first?

(They all look at each other expectantly.)

Tracey: I think it's whoever spins the highest, right?

John: Would you all mind if I just didn't play? I think I'd rather watch *20/20*.

Tracey: John! Come on.

Kris: OK, where's my stash? Ooh! $20,000—a lawyer's salary.

Kyle: Don't spend it all in one place.

(Kyle laughs and pays her the fake money.)

Tracey: It's kind of an old game.

John: Tonight on *20/20* we'll look at how you'll never make enough money—no matter what job you have—and you'll die broke, miserable, and bored.

Kyle: Or…tune into *Comedy Central* for John's life story, titled "Mr. Positive."

(They all reprove John's attitude.)

Kris: John, did you ever think that maybe your attitude affects your life? Have you ever considered that all your negativity may be why your life is…

John: Is what?

Tracey: Well, just a little left of happy. I really believe that how we think and speak affects our reality.

John: That's so…weird!

(Kyle then spins and moves.)

Kyle: Ha-ha! Check it out: he rolls a 10! Rock me baby! (*Picking up a card and reading it aloud*) Oh man, I'm gonna have to have that tattoo removed.

John: That'll leave a mark. Pay up.

(*Tracey spins and advances.*)

Tracey: Hmmm.

Kris: Now wait. Remember that if you go that way, the most you can make is $8,000 a year.

Kyle: Hello, poverty, here you come (*toward Tracey*). We'll visit you in the poorhouse.

Kris: If you go the college route, you can make more money.

John: Hah! That's a laugh.

Kyle: How come there aren't any spaces on here about having to pay back college loans?

Tracey: I told you it was an old game.

John: Yeah, twenty years ago people could actually afford school.

(*Kris advances. It's John's turn.*)

John: Okay, baby. Ah…lucky seven! (*Suddenly upset*) No way!

(*They all ask what he landed on. John slumps back in his chair, clearly upset.*)

John: Ticked the boss off, go back to start!

Kyle: I can't see you doing that.

(*They all laugh at him.*)

John: No way man, that's not fair!

Tracey: Hey, babe, watch what you say to the old man.

John: I hate this game.

Kris: Well it's *life* John. The game of *life*.

Kyle: Yeah, but real life is more complex than running around with four kids in the back seat all the time. What a drag.

Tracey: Well, I still think that what happens has a lot to do with how you think, what you tell yourself.

John: Well, little miss philosophy major…

Kris: She's right, John. Your brain and your mouth are the most powerful tools you have.

Kyle: That's bad news for John. (*All laugh.*) Have you two been watching too much daytime television again?

John: So what your saying is that everything I think and say—and virtually every move I make—has some kind of ongoing life of its own?

Kyle: *(referring to the question)* Payday!! You did say you wanted more control of your life, didn't you, John? What more do you want?

John: Look, I'm sorry. It's just this…I don't know. I guess this game has made me stop and think about things. I mean look at it. You spend the whole game in your little car, drive all over the freaking planet, do this and that, collect all this money, and hope you don't run out of money or spin a bad number. You make yourself completely insane—and for what? Just so someone else can get to the mansion first?

Kyle: "Mr. Positive" pipes up again.

John: Think about it. Doesn't it depress you to think that maybe life could be just like this game? That there's nothing you and I can do to alter it one way or the other?

Kyle: *(toward Tracey)* Have you filled his Prozac® prescription lately?

Tracey: You're the only person I know who can be so serious about a stupid board game.

(John is not amused.)

John: All I'm saying is that there should be more to it.

Tracey: To what, the game?

John: To everything.

Tracey: Maybe there is.

John: You know what, Tracey? I don't want a life where everything is left to chance, a roll of the dice. I'd like a life where my choices counted, where my words and thoughts *could* make a difference.

Kris: But it *is* like that John. Life, I mean. Every move you make!

Kyle: She's right, you know.

(Lights dim. End drama.)

Message and Prayer

Speaker   **"Every Move You Make"**

Sermon light set; project speaker; project graphics on cue.

Communion

Host with pastors assisting

Will those who are serving today please come to receive the bread and cup?

All are invited to experience communion today. The servers will stand in front of each section on the floor and to the sides in the balcony. Beginning with the front rows, each of you is invited to come, break off a piece of bread, and then dip it into the cup. When you are finished, circle back around to your seat.

The altar in front is open in front to anyone who would like to come and pray. Let us now receive the Living Word.

Featured Music

Band and Female Vocalist   "Take My Life"

Project graphic or live altar shots onscreen; lights on floor if possible.
Continue music throughout.

Sending Out

Host or Speaker

Lighting as before; project speaker onscreen.

In the real game of life, every move you make can potentially be used by God. Go this week, and let your thoughts, words, and actions pave the way to your irresistible future. Amen.

Exit Music

Band   "Take My Life"

As before, with graphic projected onscreen.

Celebration

19

The Real Jesus

THE REAL JESUS.

Felt Need: To know how the truth about Jesus can make a difference in our lives

Desired Outcome: To live our lives in light of who Jesus really is

Theme: The Real Jesus

Word: Romans 1:25

Metaphor/Image: A driver's license with Jesus' "stats" on it

The Lesson: How easy it is to create our own picture of who we want Jesus to be—and he usually ends up looking very much like us! More than ever, we must be clear about who Jesus really was, and what he was (is) really like. Only as we know "The Real Jesus" can we be equipped to introduce others to him.

The Look: Using a driver's license metaphor was a great place to start for this theme of "identifying" the real Jesus. To emphasize the idea of discovering who Jesus is, we used a silhouette on the driver's license graphic. We also created a variety of different silhouette and profile images using large pieces of black-on-blue foamboard, not only to imitate the screen graphic, but also to suggest that Jesus could have looked many different ways. These were placed strategically around the stage and floor, using easels where necessary.

Worship Celebration

Play designated CD and project main graphic; continue pre-celebration lighting.

Opening Music

Band   **"Don't You Forget About Me"**

Light band; project graphics. (These could be silhouettes similar to those described in "The Look" on the previous page.)

Video

On the Street   **"What Does Jesus Look Like?"**

Lower house lights; begin immediately following band. Video available on The Visual Edge *from (Group Publishing).*

Call to Worship

Host

Light host and project onscreen until cue (*), then project the main graphic. Have host hold up her or his driver's license.

When someone asks to see your driver's license, do you feel funny about how much personal information they will see? Your height and weight, eye color, and blood type are all there in black and white. The details *do* matter.

*What do you think the real Jesus was like? Was he tall? Dark? Handsome? Heavy-set or thin? A Democrat? A Conservative? A blue-collar worker? A CEO?

Without seeing a driver's license or a resume, it's easy to form our own picture of Jesus based on what we *want* him to be. People have been doing that for a long time. In Romans 1:25, Paul describes the sinful way that we trade the worship of the true god for that of a false god: "...[they] worshiped the god they made instead of the God who made them" (*The Message*). What a shame it would be to go through life serving a fake god, one made up in our heads!

We come together in worship to discover who Jesus really is. Only then can we authentically give our lives to being the Christ-followers we claim to be. We want to know *The Real Jesus.

Let's stand and worship together.

Song Celebration

Band   **"I Love to Praise Him"**

Light band; project words.

Prayer

Host or Musician   **"Open the Eyes of My Heart"**

Project words onscreen; light band; music continues in the background. Host ad libs prayer.

Mission Moment Video

Host introduces

Light host, then lower lighting for video; begin video on cue from floor. Tape a mission team at work.

Follow-Up and Announcements

Host

Light host and project onscreen; then project graphic.

Offerings and Featured Music

Band and Female Vocal   **"Keep the Rocks Silent"**

Light band and choir, and project them onscreen.

Message

Speaker   **"The Real Jesus"**

Light sermon area; project with graphics. Select video clip from Malcolm X *where Malcolm, in a small chapel setting, explains his faith in an extremely articulate way to the presiding clergyman.*

Wordless Drama

5 Players (can be from Band)   **"I Am Crucified With Christ"**

Lower lights; softly play "Oh Lord, You're Beautiful" on piano.

Lights up on one figure, a young man who is impersonating Christ. He simply spreads his arms and hangs his head as though hanging on the cross, lifeless. Three people come by who have props indicating who they are and what is important to them. These can be almost anyone, but should adequately represent those in the audience: i.e. a student with a backpack and book; a baseball, football, basketball, or golf player; a businessman or woman in a suit with a briefcase and cell phone, etc. Each one approaches the Christ figure individually, spots Jesus, and proceeds to put Jesus into his or her own "shape" by placing the prop (book, ball, briefcase, cell phone, etc.) in Jesus' hands, and posing him. When satisfied that Jesus is in his or her own shape, each nods in affirmation and exits, one after the other. After each person exits, Jesus returns to his original position on the cross.

One last person comes in. He or she sees Christ, and circles him curiously to inspect who he really is. After some thought, he or she stands directly in front of Jesus and assumes Jesus' position, arms outstretched and head down. As a final gesture, Jesus unexpectedly reaches out to hold the persons arms in place. (Lights fade.)

Sending Out

Speaker

Light speaker.

Exit Music

Band   "Don't You Forget About Me"

Project graphic only.

Celebration

20

Food for the Soul

Food for the Soul

Felt Need: To satisfy our spiritual hunger

Desired Outcome: To find nourishment in Jesus, the Bread of Life

Theme: Food for the Soul

Word: John 6:35

Metaphor/Image: Cookout food

The Lesson: We all have hunger: physical hunger that we're constantly aware of, and spiritual hunger that we most likely are not as aware of. This celebration introduces Jesus as the ultimate Bread of Life, and suggests that our God-hunger could be more closely related to our food-hunger than we ever knew. Humans need food—God-food!

The Look: For the graphics, we incorporated a simple mustard and ketchup color scheme with illustrations of food to create the cookout theme for this celebration. For the drama set, we used a barbeque grill (with real hamburgers!), utensils, a small table covered with a red-and-white checked tablecloth, and mustard and ketchup. This was a fun way to illustrate a vital truth.

113

Worship Celebration

Pre-celebration lighting; play selected CD before opening.

Opening Music

Band   "More Than You Know"

Light band and project onscreen.

Call to Worship and Drama

Host and Chef Gucciano   "Food for Thought"

Light host and project; then light drama area for Chef and project.

Host: God is much more than we could ever know. And that's a good thing because most days we'll take *all* we can get.

(Chef Gucciano enters and interrupts, singing. He speaks with an Italian accent and pretends to be cooking at the grill.)

Host: Well, if it isn't our old friend, Chef Gucciano. Chef, are you ready with more "Food for Thought?"

Chef: Oh, indeed I am. Today I have much food for thought, and I will make for you my famous Gucci burger with a delicious twist of my own Gucci sauce. Add corn on de cob and potato salad, and you have a complete meal that will satisfy de taste buds of de most discriminating palate. You agree?

Host: Well sure, Chef, but this is our weekly worship celebration. I'm sure I'm not the only one wondering why we're having a cooking show.

Chef: Well, I must tell you dat wherever you go, people are always hungry. Oh sure, des people might have already eaten, but I guarantee you dat in 3 hours de be hungry again. It's only human.

Host: No offense, Chef, but here at church we usually talk about what's in our heart and our soul, not in our stomach.

Chef: Of course! But de soul is so very much like de stomach. It also needs nourishment. And you can't just fill it once; it needs to be fed regularly.

Host: And so?

Chef: And so you do not just need de Gucci burger for de stomach. You also need food for de soul.

Host: And I suppose you want to share a recipe for the soul with us?

Chef: No, I will leave dat to the speaker. For now, just remember: everyone gets hungry.

Host: *(To the audience)* You may have come feeling a little hungry yourself. The good news about today's menu is that it's "all you can eat." Jesus referred to himself as the Bread of Life, who will never leave you hungry. Let's stand and celebrate his nourishing and life-giving presence.

Song Celebration

Band   **"Celebrate Jesus"**

Light band; project words onscreen.

Prayer

Musician vocal   **"I Need You More"**

Play soft music under; project graphic onscreen.

Mission Moment Video

Host

Host introduces and follows up the video. Tape a mission or ministry team at work.

Announcements

Speaker

Light speaker before and after video; project graphic onscreen.

Offerings and Featured Music

Band   **"A Song for Jesus" (aka "A Song for Mama")**

Light band and project onscreen.

Message and Storytelling

Speaker   **"Food for the Soul"**

Use this storytelling section as an opening for the message or use it in the middle.
Lower house lights; project graphics.

From John 6:

One day after crossing the Sea of Galilee, Jesus and his followers went ashore, climbed a hill, and sat down to talk together. A huge crowd, attracted by the miracles they had seen Jesus do, followed them.

What do you do when the crowd comes, there's nothing to eat, the nearest grocery is miles away, and stomachs are starting to growl?

Philip checks his wallet, while Andrew checks out the crowd. Nobody has any real food, except one little boy who's mom had remembered to pack him a lunch. Still, it wasn't much to work with. But Jesus looked at the boy's fish sandwich, and saw the ingredients for a feast. Jesus gave thanks to God, then the disciples began to pass the bread and fish around. The Bible says that everyone ate as much as they wanted; yet they had twelve baskets of leftovers. Clearly, this was one of Jesus' biggest miracles, and a definite crowd-pleaser!

Jesus was pretty smart about people, and knew that the hunger in their hearts was bigger than the hunger in their stomachs. They needed food for their souls.

Early the next day, the crowd set off to find Jesus, and found him back on the other side of the sea. When they got there, Jesus said to them, "It's nice to see you all again, but I'd guess that you're here because of the food. Let me give you a little advice: don't waste your energy working for food that will eventually get moldy in the back of your fridge! Work for the food that will stick with you always—food for the soul."

The people were growing excited: "Yeah! That's what we want! Bread from God all the time!" Jesus said, "It's *me*. I am the Bread of Life. Believe in me and you'll be fed forever."

Exit Music

Band   **"More Than You Know"**

Light band; project graphic.

Celebration

21

Where Everybody Knows My Name

Felt Need: To belong to an authentic community

Desired Outcome: To move beyond merely attending church to belonging to a church community.

Theme: Where Everybody Knows My Name

Word: Acts 2:43; Ephesians 2

Metaphor/Image: A Cheers-type sign

The Lesson: One reason the TV show, *Cheers*, was such a long-standing hit was that it touched a huge need inside every one of us—the need to belong to an authentic community. This celebration, which works also well for a graduation weekend, addresses that God-given desire inside us all.

The Look: For the main graphic, we capitalized on the look of the familiar TV show. Simple rows of chairs created the drama set while the communion elements were displayed on another area of the stage. The theme song from *Cheers* was a real connection piece for the entire celebration.

Featured Option: Communion; Graduation Affirmation

Worship Celebration

Pre-celebration lighting; play CD before start of celebration.

Opening Music

Band	***Cheers* theme song**

Light band and project onscreen.

Drama

2 Female Players	**"Where Everybody Knows Your Name"**

Shift lights to drama area; do not mute band; project players onscreen.

(Two high school girls dressed in cap and gown are seated next to each other at their graduation ceremony. Three male grads are seated behind them, jabbing each other and just keeping movement going to create the true feel of a graduation ceremony.)

Heidi: (*yawning*) Keep me awake, Angie. I'm gonna fall off my chair if I close my eyes again.

Angie: Yep, it's boring, all right. But hey, that's high school for you.

Heidi: Tell me about it. It doesn't get any slower than 5th period English Lit with Mrs. Marquette. I planned my whole wedding during that class.

Angie: I didn't know you were engaged!

Heidi: I'm not, but when I meet the right guy, I'll be ready.

Angie: Uh-huh! Yeah, high school's had its negative moments, but getting out of here could have its drawbacks, too.

Heidi: Really?

Angie: Yeah. Face it. Next year we'll be freshman again in places where no one's ever heard of us. In college you're a major, not a name. The best you can hope for is a roommate who sleeps alone and doesn't like country music.

Heidi: Sounds depressing. Maybe that's why kids join groups like sororities. It gives them a place to belong, somebody to spend time with. Even my Grandma has a card club, and my Grandpa's in the Kiwanis.

Angie: Well, no sorority for me, thanks. Still, I'd like to have a group to hang out with. It would help me feel a lot more secure.

Heidi: Yeah, it's fun to think about leaving home…but I'll never outgrow the need to be in a place where everybody knows my name.

(Fade to black. Play music tag.)

Music Tag

Band	***Cheers* theme song**

as before

Call to Worship

Host

Light speaker and project onscreen; then project graphic on cue (*).

No matter what you call it—touching base, making a connection, hanging together, doing the family thing—we all have an inner need to belong. We gravitate toward a group of people who will provide a safe space for us, and who will love us unconditionally.

As Christians we are called to be in community as the body of Christ. You can't be a Christian alone: you must be in community. Christianity is a team sport. Today we have a fresh chance to explore what it looks like when we're not just going to church, but living together in a biblical community *where everybody knows your name. Let's stand and celebrate as the community of Christ.

Song Celebration

Band   **"We've Come to Praise You"**
"What We've Come Here For"
"We've Come to Praise You" (Tag)

Mission Moment Video

Lower lights; begin video immediately. Use this as an opportunity to introduce a connection ministry such as a singles' ministry, a young adult group, or another small group.

Announcements

Host

Light speaker; project graphics.

Featured Music and Prayer

Band and Host   **"Sunscreen Remake"**

Host begins, then music; light band and Host.

"Sunscreen" is a popular song for graduates. We used the "vibe" of the original recording and added our own words from the beatitudes.

To the class of (*year*) and any others who believe that they are always on their way to a miracle.

Life won't always be easy. When you get out on your own, the day will come when you think you have reached the end of your rope, and you won't know what to do. But it's when you lose things that seemed irreplaceable, that you'll feel the full embrace of God's arms around you.

Allow yourself to feel rich without money. Contentment is being happy with just who you are—no more, no less. And it's at that contented moment that you'll find you really do possess everything you could ever want.

Make *yes* your favorite word. Discover your astounding appetite for God. God is the best meal you'll ever eat.

Never be ashamed to care deeply about someone or something. It's those who truly care for others that find themselves truly cared for.

And it's when you line up your heart and your mind with God that you'll be able to really see God alive in your world.

If you can pull people together to live side by side in harmony, the leader in you will rise to the top and you'll begin to understand your place in God's family. If your full commitment to God irritates somebody, it should only drive you deeper into God's Kingdom. And God is smiling for you. All of heaven applauds when you tell the truth about God. So amaze yourself.

There's a reason you're here. It's to be salt that brings out the God-flavors of the planet. If *you* can't be salt, how will it ever happen? No matter what your occupation, the salt-thing is why you're here.

And light. Since God is not a secret to be kept, you need to go public with God's message like a city on top of a hill. Be with people, laugh with them, talk to them, cry with them—be generous with your life. That will prompt others to open up to God, our big-hearted Father in heaven.

Soon, if not already, you're going to hear a lot about looking out for yourself, giving people what they deserve—but that really won't get you anywhere. Transform negatives. Even if someone takes you to court and sues you for the shirt off your back, gift wrap your best jeans and send them along as well. Always invent new ways to love.

Even love your enemies. Send a love letter to someone you don't like. Let them bring out the best in you, not the worst. And pray hard, because it's then that you'll be working out of your true self, you're God-created self.

That's really what God is about, after all. God always gives the best—the sun and the rain—to everyone, good and bad, nice and nasty. And that's the kind of love we are asked to share: unconditional, wild, and strong.

It's a call to grow up. You *are* kingdom subjects after all. A new community called to offer your world a new culture of love and forgiveness. It's your God-created identity, and you're just the ones to live it out.

And whatever you do, believe that you are always on your way to a miracle.

Adapted from *The Message*, pp.18-19; 21-22. Based on Matthew 5:3-16; 29-44.

Message

Speaker   "Where Everybody Knows My Name"

Light speaker.

Communion and Graduate Recognition

Speaker and Band   "Shine on Us"

Have communion onstage for all grads; project onscreen as possible.

Sending Out

Host

as before

Closing Music

Band   *Cheers* **theme song**

Light band; project graphic.

Celebration

22

Clean Slate

Felt Need: We get bogged down with guilt and need a fresh start.

Desired Outcome: To believe that God forgives and gives new direction

Theme: Clean Slate

Word: Acts 2:38

Metaphor/Image: Etch-A-Sketch®

The Lesson: As the opening video clip from *City Slickers* reminds us, everybody needs a "do-over." We've all got issues, flaws, and past events that have crowded and conflicted the screen of our lives. The good news is that Christ offers us a clean slate, a fresh start. The popular children's toy, the Etch-A-Sketch, provided a powerful visual image of wiping the slate clean.

The Look: We arranged about ten Etch-A-Sketches on black boxes for the stage display. The major connection piece, however, was a personalized primitive Etch-A-Sketch we designed for every person—pieces of red tag board with knobs printed on each one. We then added a white sticker to each red square for the screen. During the prayer we identified and wrote on our screens what we most needed to resolve in our life. At the end of the message, persons had the opportunity to peel off the stickers, and place them on an old wooden cross, lying on its side. We also set up several stations where adults had the opportunity to reaffirm their baptisms. The result was a powerful and truly life-changing worship celebration.

Featured Options: Adult Baptism or Reaffirmation of Baptism

Worship Celebration

Play pre-celebration CD.

Opening

Video Clip   **from *City Slickers***

Lower house lights; begin playing clip immediately. Play scene where Billy Crystal's character tells Daniel Stern's character that even though he's messed up his whole life, everyone gets a "do-over."

Opening Music

Band   **"Starting Over"**

Light band; project Etch-A-Sketch animation (available on MSWII resource).

Call to Worship

Host

Host carries an Etch-A-Sketch.
Light speaker and project onscreen; show main graphic on cue(*).

Do you recall the first time you ever played with an Etch-A-Sketch? I do. I was fascinated with being able to draw without a pencil by using just those two knobs. I'd try all sorts of curves and designs, until sooner or later I would mess up and want to start over. And that's where the magic came in, because all you have to do to start over is... *(Host allows audience to respond and vigorously shakes the Etch-A-Sketch to erase the drawing.)*

In the big Etch-A-Sketch of life, we can reach the point where the picture of our life is a tangled and confused jumble. But out of our sense of shame, we just keep turning knobs, trying to hide the inevitable. Jesus' answer for us is to wipe the *slate clean *(host turns etch-a-sketch over and shakes it)*, so that we can start fresh and allow God to do something new and creative in our lives. That's good news for us bad artists!

Celebrate with us now as we stand and sing.

Song Celebration

Band   **"Where Do I Go?"**
                                            "Sweet Mercies"
                               "Create in Me a Clean Heart"

Light band; project words.

Prayer with Etch-A-Sketch Cards

Host

Seat host on stool; light host and band softly; project graphic.
Band continues with soft music as necessary, playing "Create in Me a Clean Heart" at end.

Something about seeing an Etch-A-Sketch makes you want to get your hands on it and start doodling. When you mess up, all you do is turn it over and shake it, and you have a fresh start.

Today we're talking about fresh starts, clean slates. All of you received a replica of an Etch-A-Sketch. We are going to use it now as a part of our prayer.

If you were to ask God for a fresh start today, what would you most need to resolve before that would be possible? Is there one thing—an issue, a relationship, an addiction, a habit, or a dependence—that would have to go? Write on your Etch-A-Sketch a word, a symbolic letter, or something that describes your unclean slate to God. After the message, you'll have the opportunity to peel off the sticker to clean the slate. You can then place the stickers on the cross—if you so choose—as a sign that we are turning over to God what we can't heal about ourselves.

Let's pray together:

> God, even though we love you, sometimes an issue, a habit, or an addiction paralyzes us, and stands between who we are and who you call us to be. We can't serve something else and you. We want to name it today, Lord. Help us to let go of it, and to trust that you will be there to help us resolve it. Lord, help us to be faithful and honest with what we know about ourselves, and hopeful and trusting of what we know about you. We know you are awesome, holy, always good, and a friend of the those who mess up. Take our lives today, Lord, and be our Redeemer. In the name of Jesus, who died that we might live anew. Amen.

Announcements and Offerings

Host

Light host and project with graphics.

Featured Music

Band   "Show Me the Way"

Light band and project onscreen.

Message

Speaker   "A Clean Slate"

Light speaker.

Adult Baptism or Reaffirmation

Speaker introduces

Jazz introduction of "I Surrender All"; light floor if possible.

Sending Out

Host

as before

Exit Music

Band   "Show Me the Way"

as before

Celebration 23

Hello, My Name Is

Felt Need: We need a God who is bigger than any challenge we can face.

Desired Outcome: To trust God in our "impossible" circumstances

Theme: Hello, My Name Is

Word: Exodus 3:1-14

Metaphor/Image: Stick-on nametags

The Lesson: We are anxious people. We run around trying to anticipate, alleviate, and negate the disastrous outcomes of everyday situations. We're invited to relax in the care of a God who promises to be the "I Am" of every situation. Just like Moses, we need the freedom to "namedrop" the title of the One whose coverage and care is bigger than our circumstance.

The Look: For this celebration, we provided everyone with nametags. During the prayer, we encouraged people to write on the nametags the word that most described who they needed God to be at that time. We invited people to take their nametags home as a reminder of God's presence in each unique situation. Candle stands, a cross, and the communion elements were used to create the display for this communion celebration.

Featured Option: Communion

Worship Celebration

Play an acoustic CD; use pre-celebration lighting.

Opening Music

Band   "Name"

Light band and project onscreen.

Storytelling and Call to Worship

Host or Storyteller   Exodus 3:1-14

Light speaker; project graphics.

Moses was a man who didn't want anyone to know his name. After committing a crime in Egypt, he'd fled deep into the desert to lay low. He settled in the land of Midian; married Zipporah, the daughter of the priest of Midian; and tended his father-in-law's flock of sheep.

One day while Moses was out with the flock, he went beyond the wilderness and came to Horeb, the mountain of God. He suddenly came upon a bush in the distance with a flame coming up out of the middle.

"Too much desert time," Moses thought, as he rubbed his eyes and smacked himself. "I've really got to get a life here." As he walked closer to the bush he could see that none of the bush was being consumed, yet the fire blazed brightly from the middle.

"Moses, Moses!" God called from inside the bush.

You can imagine that Moses was pretty freaked out at being on a first-name basis with a bush!

"Here I am," Moses replied.

"Not so fast." God said. "Take off your sandals. That place where you are standing is holy ground."

Holy ground? Moses did not yet know that God loved to show up in the mundane spots—like bushes, bedrooms, and feeding troughs.

It took a little processing time, but once Moses understood that this really was God talking, he hid his face in fear.

"Moses," God said, "Look, I've seen more suffering than you can imagine. I have heard the cry of my people in their slavery and oppression. I've come to lead them out of Egypt and to a land of their own, a land of plenty. I'm sending you to Pharaoh to demand their release."

"God, no! I mean, who am I? Not even your people will believe me, let alone Pharaoh. Who will I tell them sent me? What will I say? 'Hello, my name is Moses?' Come on God, I need connections. References. I need a name."

"I AM who I AM. Tell them 'I AM' sent you."

Because, you see, I AM says it all. I AM is everything we could ever want for anything we could ever need. We've come to celebrate the great I AM: the one who led the Israelites out of Egypt; the one who said "I will be your God, and you will be my people"; the one who died on a cross to show us the depth of his love.

Let us stand to sing and lift God's name on high.

Song Celebration

Band   **"Lord I Lift Your Name on High"**
                                                      "Yes, Lord"

Light band; project words.

Prayer

Host

Play soft music under; light host; project graphic.

Who is it that you need God to be at this moment in time? A provider, a healer, a Savior, or a friend? Take a moment and write on your nametag who you need God to be for you right now. Let's pray:

> Lord, there are times when circumstances overwhelm us, and we know ourselves to be totally inadequate for the task at hand. That's when you say, "Good. Now *I* can work!" You calm our anxieties when you announce, "I AM. I am all you need." Lord, today we humbly ask for faith to trust ourselves and our anxieties to your care. Amen.

Song of Response

Band   **"Worship You"**

Project words onscreen.

Mission Moment Video

Host introduces

Light host; lower lights and begin video. Consider creating a unique ministry mission video.

Announcements

Host

Light host; project host and graphics.

Offerings and Featured Music

Band   "You Are God"

Light band and project onscreen.

Message

Speaker   "Hello, My Name Is...God"

Light speaker.

Communion

Host with assisting Pastors

Host or pastor gives instructions.

Communion is the moment in time where each one of us can bring ourselves—our fears, our anxieties, our burdens, our mistakes—to God. Will those who are serving today please come at this time?

Band   "From This Moment"

Light band; project band along with candles, bread, etc.

Sending Out

Host

Light speaker; continue instrumental music.

God is really much bigger than we can know and experience. As you go this week, remember that God is always present and available to be everything you need. Amen.

Exit Music

Band   "From This Moment"

Light band and project graphic.

Celebration
24
Extreme Courage

Felt Need: We feel fearful about acting out our faith.

Desired Outcome: To practice a fearless lifestyle

Theme: Extreme Courage

Word: Acts 4

Metaphor/Image: Cross

The Lesson: Some people seem to possess more courage than others, but in reality none of us are truly fearless. The brave have simply learned how to work through their fears, and act instead on what they know to be true. Acts 4 depicts a band of post-resurrection followers of Christ who, through the power given to them at Pentecost, were able to make powerful and courageous witness to what they had experienced of Christ. We too have been given the gift of the Holy Spirit so that we might have "Extreme Courage" to act out God's call and purpose on earth.

The Look: We used the cross as the metaphor for Christ's extreme courage. The graphic for this celebration was created by substituting a stylized cross for the "X" in the word *Extreme*. For the stage display, we placed a large wooden cross on its side and at an angle so that it resembled an "X." We then surrounded the cross with candle stands.

Featured Option: New Members

Worship Celebration

Play a CD before the beginning of the service.

Opening Video

from *Wizard of Oz*

Lower house lights; begin on cue from floor. Show scene where the Lion tells Dorothy that he wants to obtain courage from the Wizard.

Opening Music

Band   "I Go to Extremes"

Light band and project onscreen.

Call to Worship

Host

Light host; project host and graphics on cue (*).

Christianity is a call to extreme courage. Have you ever known someone who, despite danger or unpopular opinion, just went right on and said or did the right thing? Circumstances might not have been favorable, but that person simply did what needed to be done, without thought for his or her own well-being.

We all can think of examples of people who have displayed this kind of courage: *Abraham Lincoln, *Martin Luther King, Jr., *Mother Teresa. And what about the disciples? They defied the authorities and were arrested for preaching about the life and resurrection of Jesus.

What do these people have that we don't have? *Extreme courage. "Courage," said the cowardly lion, "can make a slave into a King." With courage, lives that are bland and boring can become fearless and fiery. As Christians, we are called to boldly and courageously live our faith. Let's stand together and sing these songs of faith.

Song Celebration

Band   "What a Mighty God"
"Dance Like David"

Light band; project words onscreen.

Transition/Prayer

Host

Daring acts of faith would be a great thing to be able to do, but most of us would be happy to have courage enough to boldly live out the Christ-life each day at home and work.

Where do you lack courage? If you felt no fear, what would you do differently tomorrow morning? Would you talk to someone openly about your faith? Take a class to improve your job skills? Would you break off a destructive relationship, or perhaps give up something you're not sure you can live without?

We all need courage. If we had more of it, we'd be setting the world on fire. We definitely need to live more boldly, more courageously. I invite you to listen to these words of comfort and assurance.

Host and Vocalists

Light and project speakers as possible; play soft music under.

Vocalist 1: "Friends, when life gets really difficult, don't jump to the conclusion that God isn't on the job. Instead, be glad that you are in the very thick of what Christ experienced." (1 Peter 4:12-13, *The Message*)

Vocalist 2: "None of this fazes us because Jesus loves us. I'm absolutely convinced that nothing—nothing living or dead, angelic or demonic, today or tomorrow, thinkable or unthinkable—absolutely *nothing* can get between us and God's love because of the way that Jesus our Master has embraced us." (Romans 8:38-39, *The Message*)

Vocalist 3: "Do not fear, for I am with you; do not be afraid, for I am your God; I will strengthen you, and I will help you; I will uphold you with my victorious right hand." (Isaiah 41:10, *NIV*)

Vocalist 2: "When you pass through the waters, I will be with you; and when you pass through the rivers, they will not sweep over you. When you walk through the fire, you will not be burned; the flames will not set you ablaze." (Isaiah 43:2, *NIV*)

Vocalist 3: "Whatever I have, wherever I am, I can make it through anything in the One who makes me who I am." (Philippians 4:13, *The Message*)

Host: Lord, we look to you today for what you must give us. Thank you for your promises that you cannot break. Hear our prayer as we sing now.

Prayer Song

Band   "We Fall Down"

Light band; project words onscreen.

Announcements

Host

Light host and project intermittently with graphics.

Membership

Host or Pastor

Continue lighting host; also light new members if possible.
Project new members and graphic as necessary.

Recently a number of real followers here took the courageous next step to complete our membership course and have prepared to covenant with us to become members of this community. As they stand before us now, let's join in dialog together as we affirm our commitment to one another and to God.

Brothers and sisters in Christ, you have worked together, played together, studied together, and prayed together, and right now your desire is to covenant with this community of believers as members—fully devoted followers. Please answer these questions as a testimony of your intentions:

Do you intend to participate fully in this community through your prayers, your presence, your gifts and your service? (*I do.*)

And do you courageously state that as a real follower of Christ and his mission that you will serve as a representative of Jesus to the world? (*I do.*)

And congregation, do you affirm the gifts these people bring to this place of community, and do you invite and welcome the Spirit of God that rests on them? If so say, "We do." (*We do.*)

Membership Prayer

Host or Pastor

God, we welcome these followers here in your name. We know they are yours, God. We ask you not to protect or preserve us *from* the world, but to send us *out* to the world as revolutionaries, daring to be the Kingdom of God to a world that waits to see the real thing. By the power of your Spirit, give us the courage to boldly live our faith. We trust ourselves to you. Amen.

Let's welcome these people. (*applause*)

As part of their faith journey, many of these people were baptized last week and we'll re-experience that event in a moment on the screen. (*Play video during offering.*) We take time to give now, willingly and freely as an act of worship. Listen to this song of courage as the ushers come.

Offerings and Featured Music

Band and Female Vocal   **"Carry Me High"**

Light band; play baptism video, if available.

Message

Speaker   **"Extreme Courage"**

Light speaker.

Sending Out

Host

Lighting as before.

Exit Music

Band   **"Carry Me High" (chorus)**

Lighting as before.

Celebration
25
Following Ancient Paths

Following Ancient Paths

Felt Need: Organized religion isn't working for us.

Desired Outcome: To find new meaning and power through the simple truth of Jesus

Theme: Following Ancient Paths

Word: 1 John 2:7-8; Jeremiah 6:16

Metaphor/Image: Large stones; landmarks on the path

The Lesson: Faith itself cannot be transmitted through the institutions of organized religion. It must be demonstrated through an authentic community that lives out the unique call of God in a particular location. Identifying the inadequacies of institutional church helps us to be sure of our own mandate: to follow ancient paths whose two markers are identified as Jesus and the embodiment of love.

The Look: Several pieces make this a high-engagement celebration. The "On the Street" video asks everyday people, "Why do you or don't you go to church?" The responses are amazingly helpful and draw the audience in immediately. The metaphor of ancient paths and landmarks was visually achieved by placing rocks (real or imitation) on the stage. In addition, each person received a small, smooth stone with the word *Jesus* printed on it in permanent marker as a constant reminder of what the church must be about.

Worship Celebration

Play a CD of Celtic music.
Use pre-celebration lighting with gobos of stained glass windows.

Opening Music

Band   **"If I Ever Lose My Faith"**

Light band and project onscreen.

Video

On the Street   **"Why Church?"**

Lower lights; video available on The Visual Edge *(Group Publishing).*

Reprise Song

Band   **"If I Ever Lose My Faith"**

as before

Call to Worship

Host and 3 Speakers   **"Institutionally Incorrect"**

Speakers up at beginning; light drama area for host and 3 speakers.

Charlie Brown once said that "he loved mankind; it was people he couldn't stand." Likewise, you and I might say that we love God, but it's the Church we struggle with. In the new millennium, will it be possible to have our deepest needs met within the context of the organized church? Has anyone here ever felt frustrated with institutionalized religion?

Have the host and speakers discuss childhood or early church experiences that were negative. Ask them not to mention specific names and places, but to anonymously discuss how organized religion has been detrimental to their faith.

Transition to Prayer

Host

Church can be a place where we experience deep pain. It can also be a place where we experience life-changing grace.

In ancient times, without the luxury of roadways, large rocks would be used as markers to chart one's course or path. Today we want to rediscover the road markers, the unmovable truths of God, that will help us to chart our course so that we may find new meaning and power in our lives.

Hear these words from Jeremiah (6:16):

> Stand at the crossroads and look;
> ask for the ancient paths,
> ask where the good way is, and walk in it
> and you will find rest for your souls.

Will you follow the ancient paths? Bow your heads as we pray together.

Prayer and Song

Host and Band Leader   "I See You"

Begin soft music under prayer; ask congregation to stand.
Host and speakers exit stage following prayer.

Band Leader: Lord God, everyone here has had unique experiences of church. For some it's always been a good experience, and we're thankful for that. But for many of us, Lord, church has been a source of pain, or at best, has been a place of indifference. We've longed to find markers for our faith, but instead have encountered fences of exclusion—walls built by others who themselves struggle.

Host: Lord, we come to you today because in our hearts we want to be a people and a place where others can experience you. Make us aware of the presence of your hand, your heart, your love, and your promises all around us. All of these are most concrete and real in Jesus, the visible presence of God, who is the embodiment of love. Help us also to be a community that embodies your love. Amen.

Begin singing "Everywhere I Go I See You."

Song Celebration

Band   "Glory to Glory"
"Everywhere I Go I See You" (Reprise)

Light band; project words onscreen.

Announcements

Host

Light host; project graphics.

Offering and Featured Song

Band and Choir (optional)   "I'm Not Afraid" (Male Vocal)

Light band and choir; project onscreen.

Message

Speaker   "Following Ancient Paths"

Light host and project; show graphics on cue.

Sending Out

Host

Light host; project graphic.

We don't need more fences to separate us or more arbitrary rocks to trip over. Help us to be the real thing: a community whose actions demonstrate your love to one another and to the world.

(Holding out the rock with Jesus *inscribed on it)* In your hand is a reminder of the only rock you'll ever need: Jesus, the embodiment of love. Go this week and be the real thing. Amen.

Exit Music

Band   "Glory to Glory"

Light band; project band or graphic onscreen.

Celebration 26

Walk on the Water

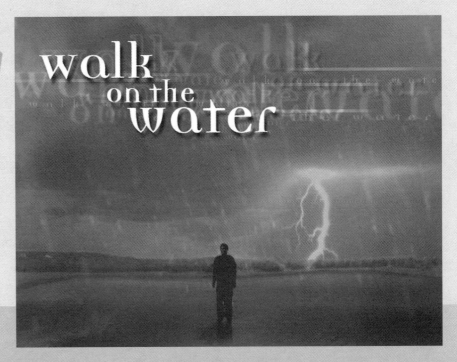

Felt Need: To let go of our need for security so we may step out in faith

Desired Outcome: To decide to take the ultimate risk toward Jesus and life!

Theme: Walk on the Water

Word: Matthew 14:22-33

Metaphor/Image: A light on the stormy water

The Lesson: This is the first of three celebrations that focus on the story of Peter walking on the water. This celebration addresses our human penchant for staying safe and dry and comfortable. When Peter responded to Jesus' call and stepped out on the water, he demonstrated a major part of faith—the willingness to be uncomfortable. It's a risk we all need to take.

The Look: For this three-week series we found a wooden rowboat and placed it on the drama area of our stage, propped it up a bit, and placed oars and a fish net inside. The storyteller used that space while the screen animation helped us visualize the action of the story. To make the celebration even more interactive, have the speaker/pastor sprinkle water on people as they file past the stage, pronouncing God's blessing on each one and encouraging them to not retreat from getting wet!

Worship Celebration

Play CD; pre-celebration lighting; backlight drama area.

Opening Video

"Walk on Water" Animation

Lower house lights; project animation onscreen. Animation available on Media Resource '99 *and* The Visual Edge *from (Group Publishing).*

Storytelling

Storyteller   "Take Courage"

Light drama area; continue projecting animation.

Immediately after the meal was finished, Jesus insisted that the disciples get in the boat and go on ahead to the other side while he dismissed the people. As the crowd dispersed, Jesus climbed the mountainside so he could be by himself and pray. He stayed there alone, late into the night.

Meanwhile, the disciples' boat was far out to sea when they encountered a storm. The wind picked up, and their boat was battered by the waves. It was about four o'clock in the morning. Suddenly, they looked up and saw Jesus walking toward them on the water. They were scared out of their wits. "A ghost!" they said, crying out in terror.

But Jesus was quick to comfort them. "Courage, it's me. Don't be afraid." Peter, suddenly bold, said: "Master, if it's really you, call me to come to you on the water."

Jesus said to Peter, "Come ahead."

(Adapted from *The Message*, Matthew 14:22-29.)

Opening Music

Band   "Walk on Water"

Light band and project onscreen.

Call to Worship

Host   "Staying Dry"

Light speaker and project; then project graphic.

It's a dark and stormy night. You're out in the boat with friends when a strange voice calls to you from the water. The voice invites you to walk on the water. What's your plan? To stay as dry as you possibly can.

Sounds a lot like your life, doesn't it? At times, things are quite dark and stormy. And occasionally you hear a voice that calls you to do what you don't think you can. So your plan is to play it safe and stay as dry as you possibly can.

Most of us are that way. We grew up with our parents warning us not to get wet: Don't step in puddles; get back from the edge of the water; come in out of the rain. And the older we get, the more determined we are to stay dry at all costs. But what are we missing? And will we ever get the chance to walk on the water?

Imagine you and me, a boat, a stormy lake, and a God who wants to take us to a new place. Let's worship.

Song Celebration

Band   **"Come, Now Is the Time"**
"Step by Step"

Light band; project words onscreen.

Storytelling B

Storyteller (cont.)   **"Out of the Boat"**

Light drama area; project storyteller and animation.
Play sound effects.

Jesus said to Peter, "Come ahead."

Jumping out of the boat, Peter began to walk on the water toward Jesus. But when he looked down at the waves churning beneath his feet, he lost his nerve and started to sink. "Master," he cried, "Save me!"

Well, Jesus didn't hesitate. He reached down and grabbed Peter's hand. Then Jesus said, "Faint-heart, what got into you?"

(Adapted from *The Message*, Matthew 14:29)

Storyteller is joined by several others for an ad libbed dialog about fear-filled experiences they have had. Host ad libs prayer to conclude.

Announcements and Mission Moment

Host   **"Kids Say Thanks"**

Light speaker and project with graphics. Video available on Media Resource '99. *This resource shows kids thanking their teachers.*

Offerings and Featured Music

Band   **"Faith of the Heart"**

Light band and project onscreen.

Message

Speaker   **"Walk on the Water"**

Light speaker and project; show graphics on cue.

Response/Sprinkling and Exit

Host

See The Look *at beginning of this celebration.*

Celebration
27

Brave Hearts

Felt Need: Hope for the storms in our lives

Desired Outcome: To courageously live out our faith

Theme: Brave Hearts

Word: Matthew 14:22-33

Metaphor/Image: Stormy water and boat (the Peter story)

The Lesson: Second in the three week "Walking on the Water" series, this celebration focuses on courage. Most of us lack the courage to fully live out God's purposes; and so, like the other eleven in the boat, we hold back, often chiding the one brave heart who is willing to step out in faith. Peter didn't walk on water because he was talented, handsome, or wealthy. Peter was crazy and courageous—and that suited Jesus just fine.

The Look: We kept the boat prop in the drama area and added a fog machine (behind and underneath the propped up boat) for added affect, especially during the storytelling. In another area, we displayed the elements for communion, complete with candles and a fish net to tie in the nautical look.

Featured Option: Communion

145

Worship Celebration

Play a CD before beginning of service. Use pre-celebration lighting; backlight drama area.
Use fog machine to produce stormy effects around boat.
Band and choir up on stage by starting time.

Opening Music

Band or Female Vocalist   **"Nevertheless"**

Lower house lights; light band and choir and project onscreen.

Storytelling

Storyteller   **from Matthew 14**

Light drama area only; show "Braveheart" animation onscreen. Animation available on Media Resource '99.

It was the middle of the night. Jesus' disciples were out at sea. A storm had erupted, and their boat was being tossed around like a toy at the mercy of the waves. Frantic, they looked out and saw a figure walking towards them across the water. They thought it was a ghost.

But it was Jesus who called to assure them. "Courage guys. It's me. Don't be afraid." Suddenly, Peter felt a surge of bravery and broke out in front of the others. "Master," he said, "If it's really you, call me and I'll come to you on the water!"

The eleven looked at Peter in disbelief. Why would he even think of doing such a thing? What a show-off!

Jesus' voice roared again over the waves, "Come ahead!"

Jumping out of the boat, Peter walked on the water toward Jesus. But when he looked down at the churning waves, fear overcame him and he started to sink. "Master!" he gasped, "Save me!"

Jesus didn't hesitate. He reached out and grabbed Peter's hand, and together they made it back to the boat.

Reprise

Band and Choir   **"Nevertheless"**

Light band and choir, and project onscreen.

Call to Worship

Host 1

Light speaker and project; project graphic on cue (*).

Have you ever wondered why Peter was the only disciple to jump out of the boat? All of the disciples had seen Jesus perform miracles. All twelve knew who Jesus claimed to be. Yet only Peter believed that Jesus' power could enable him to do the miraculous. Peter didn't walk on the water because he was talented, handsome, or wealthy. Peter got a chance to walk on the water because he was crazy and courageous. He threw caution to the wind and trusted the One he could hear but couldn't really see. *Brave hearts.

Is there a brave heart inside of you? Let us listen and respond to the One who shows up in the storm and calls out to the brave hearts.

Song Celebration

Band   "I See You"
"Glory to Glory"

Light band; project words onscreen.

Transition/Video

Host 2   A Personal Testimony

Light speaker and project; lower lights and go to video. This video should show a story of someone in the congregation who has shown courage.

Live Interview

Host 2 and person featured in video above

Light speaker; play soft music under; project graphics. In this segment, the person whose video-taped testimony has been shown is interviewed.

Announcements

Host 1

Light speaker; project graphics.

Offerings and Featured Music

Band   "Never Surrender"

Light band; project stills from testimony video if possible, then go to live projection.

Message

Speaker   **"Bravehearts"**

Light speaker and project onscreen; project graphics on cue. You might want to choose a clip from Braveheart *to show.*

Communion

Host and Band   **"Open Arms"**

Light host and band; project elements or band onscreen.

Will those serving please come now?

Through communion we are invited to taste and touch the One who first reaches out for us. This is our opportunity to respond to God's call, to venture out in faith.

"Lord, this is what you have said. It looks crazy, but I am going to venture out on your word."

As you come forward for communion, make this your response, your next step of obedience to God's call.

Sending Out (if needed)

Host 1 or Speaker

Light speaker; project graphic.

God isn't looking for talented, beautiful, or wealthy people. Instead, God calls for brave hearts who are willing to look crazy and to venture out on God's word. With perseverance, passion, and practice, you can be the one. Amen.

Exit Music

Band   **Instrumental or "Open Arms"**

as before

Celebration 28

Fragile

Felt Need: To be assured that God can and does use us in spite of our mistakes and our imperfections

Desired Outcome: To embrace my humanity and allow God to work in my life

Theme: Fragile

Word: Matthew 14:22-33

Metaphor/Image: A boat or water scene from the viewpoint of a struggling swimmer

The Lesson: The last in the three-week Peter series, this message addresses what it means to be human with all it's failures, foibles, and fragility. If our humanness could disqualify us from serving God's purpose, we'd all be sunk! The hope for us is that there is a strong arm that reaches down to grab us when we cry out in desperation, "Jesus, save me!"

The Look: To change things up a bit, we added candle stands around the boat. (See previous weeks in this series.) The combination of the message, the music, and the interactive prayer created a powerful worship experience.

Worship Celebration

Play a CD that has wind and surf sound effects on it; use pre-celebration lighting.

Video

from *Jerry McGuire*

Lower house lights. Show scene where Tom Cruise's character writes his mission statement, shows it to his boss, and then is fired.

Opening Music

Band   **"Fragile"**

Light band and project onscreen.

Call to Worship

Host

Light speaker and project onscreen; project graphic on cue (*).

Being fragile and vulnerable is not such a bad thing. It's when we think we're strong and infallible that we get into trouble. Peter was an adventurer, a risk taker, and a passionate follower of Jesus. Peter boldly stepped out on the water, responding to Jesus' call to come. But after a few successful steps, he looked down at his feet, lost his nerve, and fell into the water, choking on the words, "Master, save me!" *Of course, Jesus didn't leave him there to drown, and you have to wonder if Peter's best memory of that day was the firm hand that reached down to him when he so desperately needed it. Fragile is an OK place to be when you know someone's there to save you.

The Christian life isn't a drama, a chance to act like we have it all together. It's about discovering what it is to be fully human so we can know and trust the One who is fully God. We're free to fall. We're free to fail. We've got a God waiting to hear us say, "Master, Save me." Let that be your song today.

Songs of Confession

Band   **"Where Do I Go"**
                                                     "You Alone"

Light band; project words onscreen.

Video

from "Kids Say Thanks"

Lower house lights; begin video immediately. Show scene from "Kids Say Thanks" where it says "my teacher told me it's OK to be scared." Available on Media Resource '99.

Prayer and Response

Host   **"Jesus, Save Me"**

Light speaker and project; then project graphic for prayer with response line on cue.
Play music softly under prayer.

It's OK to fail. Failure is what happens along the way when people set out to do all they were created to do. But you and I try so hard to avoid it. We struggle to admit our own fallibility. We work hard to keep those around us from seeing our failure.

This is a simple prayer of confession for fragile followers: "Jesus, save me." When we say this prayer, we admit that we're not perfect, that we make mistakes, that trouble and tragedy could happen at any moment, and that we can't save ourselves.

As I read from Psalm 51, let's say this prayer together responsively when it appears on the screen.

> O God, may the size of Your love be the size of Your mercy. And may the amount of your mercy be enough to forgive my sins and cancel out my guilt.

Jesus, save me.

I have failed, God, and my failures weigh heavily on my heart. I can't share them all with my brothers or sisters lest they weigh too heavily upon them or even threaten our relationship. But you know what they are, God, and how far I have fallen short of You.

Jesus, save me.

I know that nothing can be hidden from You. I can only acknowledge my humanity and trust in Your loving forgiveness. Wash me of my guilt, God. Heal the hurts of those who have been harmed by my failures.

Jesus, save me.

I bring You nothing God, only a foolish and fragile heart. I come to You with a sincere desire to be Your servant, to walk in Your course for my life, to bask in Your love and reflect it to those around me.

Jesus, save me.

I thank You, God, that this is all you ask and that I will remain Your child forever. Amen.

Adapted from Leslie F. Brandt, *Psalms/Now,* © 1973 Concordia Publishing House, p. 87-88. Used by permission.

Song of Response

Band   **"I Need You More"**

Light band; project words onscreen.

Announcements

Host

Light speaker; project graphics.

Offerings and Featured Music

Band   **"What If I Stumble?"**

Light band and project onscreen.

Message

Speaker   **"Fully Human"**

Light speaker and project; show graphics on cue.

Sending Out and Response

Host

Light speaker; project graphic; play soft music under.

Exit Music

Band   **"Fragile"**

as before

Celebration

29

Traveling Mercies

TRAVELING MERCIES
the Jesus journey

Felt Need: To know how to prepare for Christ's coming into our lives

Desired Outcome: To commit to preparing for Christ's coming by self-examination

Theme: Traveling Mercies

Word: Matthew 24:37-44

Metaphor/Image: Luggage

The Lesson: Preparation is an essential step in the deployment of any great event. John the Baptist challenged the people, "Prepare ye the way of the Lord," so that the full impact of Christ's ministry could be demonstrated on earth.

Even in today's speed-driven world, special events require careful and deliberate preparation. As we embark on the Jesus journey in this season of Advent, we would do well to empty our suitcases of unnecessary baggage (sin), so that we can make room for the presence of Jesus Christ!

The Look: Suitcases were displayed in an attractive arrangement in the drama area. We used a candelabra (with 5 advent candles) as part of that arrangement, along with other candles and candle stands.

Worship Celebration

Play a Christmas jazz CD; use pre-celebration lighting.

Video Clip

From *Summer Vacation*

Lower house lights. Show scene where the Griswold family drives into the garage with the luggage still on top of the roof rack, knocking it off.

Opening Music

Band   **"Life Is a Highway"**

Trail video without audio; light band; eventually project band onscreen.

Opening Skit and Call to Worship

2 Players, 1 Female and 1 Male

Light players and project onscreen.

A young woman is standing mid-stage in an imaginary line holding a bus ticket. She is impatiently waiting her turn, and anxiously checks her watch several times. Unbeknownst to her, her suitcase has fallen open, and its contents have spilled out nearby. A young man approaches her, kindly picking up some of the fallen articles and handing them to her to repack.

MALE: Excuse me, uh…your suitcase is…

FEMALE: Oh my gosh! Give me that. I can't believe this.

MALE: Do I know…?

FEMALE: No!

MALE: Haven't I seen…?

FEMALE: No!

MALE: Can I help?

FEMALE: No!

MALE: (*Almost giving up*) You sure do have a lot of stuff. (*picking up 2 shampoo bottles*) If you don't mind me asking, why do you need regular shampoo and scalp saver? I only use…

FEMALE: Well, thank you, Vidal Sassoon, but I'm afraid I might need both. You can't always tell what you're gonna need ahead of time. And if you get there and don't have what you need, you're…

MALE: Flaky?

FEMALE: What?

MALE: Flaky, without the scalp saver, I mean. I know what you're saying.

FEMALE: Well, at last.

MALE: And I know packing isn't easy.

FEMALE: Right. It isn't. I mean, when I went to see my sister after she had her baby, I remembered everything except the one thing I needed most.

MALE: What?

FEMALE: Earplugs. Every night at 3 A.M. I heard: "Whaaa!"

MALE: Your sister?

FEMALE: No, the baby. Stay with me here, OK?

MALE: Sorry.

FEMALE: And then when my grandpa died, I thought I had packed everything, only to find out the morning of the funeral that I'd forgotten my black dress.

MALE: Black dress?

FEMALE: Yeah. You know—funerals, black, sadness?

MALE: Oh. So what'd you do?

FEMALE: What any young woman would do on such an occasion. I…

TOGETHER: Went shopping!

FEMALE: Right. Man, why won't this line move? The bus will be gone by the time I check in!

MALE: Hey, have you ever thought about…oh, wow, I don't know how to say it.

FEMALE: Go ahead. Try me.

MALE: I mean, um, if your life was a…journey, like, to see God, what would you take in your suitcase?

FEMALE: Oh, so you're one of those religious freaks who hang out at airports and bus stations and harass people about religion?

MALE: No. Really. I don't even have flowers or anything. I just thought I'd ask. Because if there's one Person you gotta get ready for, it would be God.

FEMALE: Get ready for God? I wouldn't have the faintest idea how to do that. Oh look, they're boarding now. Thanks and take care! Here, maybe you should keep the scalp saver! (*She tosses the bottle to him and leaves.*)

MALE: (*turning to audience*) Hey, know it or not, we're all on a life-journey, a trip. Now, I'm *not* a religious freak, but I do know that most people on planet earth don't have any idea how to meet God. The first time Jesus came it was a total surprise. People weren't prepared. Next time I'd like to be ready, wouldn't you? What's in your suitcase?

(*Fade out.*)

Songs Celebration

Band   **"Heaven Is in My Heart"**
                                         "Great Is Thy Faithfulness"

Light band; project words onscreen.

Advent Prayer

Host   **"O Come, O Come Emmanuel"**

Light band as before; light host. Show main graphic.

The Christian Church celebrates Advent—the four weeks before Christmas—as a season of preparation, because when something great is about to happen, we should be prepared. When you get ready for a trip, you take care to pack the right things, and try hard not to leave out anything important.

We all go to great lengths to make the holidays festive and wonderful, but as we join together in prayer, our privilege is to get prepared on the *inside* for the journey to the One who is God. Today we have lit this Advent candle to demonstrate that we want to be ready, that we want to be prepared. Let's bow together and pray:

> Lord Jesus, you are Emmanuel, God with us. In the quietness of this time, we reflect on you alone. As we prepare for the Jesus journey, we first admit that we have hearts full of unwanted baggage, suitcases full of the wrong stuff. There are sins that must go so we may be clean and ready. Each of us have unwanted baggage. Perhaps it was:

> that lie you told;
> the time you exploded in anger;
> the day you were needed but didn't respond;
> the business trip that took you *so far* away from home;
> that date;
> that jealousy;
> that habit.

> As you identify your baggage, silently confess it to God as preparation for Christ's coming.

> *(Pause for reflective time.)*

> Lord, we give you who we are. We want to begin our Jesus journey with renewed energy. Thank you for new seasons of life. Thank you for *your* life. Amen.

Mission Moment

Host introduces

Light host, then lower lights. Highlight a special Christmas outreach that your church or community is engaged in.

Announcements

Host

Light speaker; project graphics.

Offerings and Featured Music

Band   **"People Get Ready"**

Light band and project onscreen.

Message

Speaker   **"Traveling Mercies"**

Light speaker and project onscreen; show graphics on cue.

Sending Out

Host

Light host; project main graphic.

Exit Music

Band   **"Life Is a Highway"**

Light band; project main graphic.

Celebration
30
A Diligent Expedition

A Diligent EXPEDITION
the Jesus journey

Felt Need: To find God, whatever it takes

Desired Outcome: To commit to making spiritual preparations for the journey of faith

Theme: A Diligent Expedition

Word: Matthew 2—The Wise Men

Metaphor/Image: Backpacker and gear

The Lesson: The stories of the first Christmas have become so commonplace that we've lost the passion and emotion of the characters involved. Seldom have we considered the hardship that the wise men endured as they journeyed toward the Messiah. When we begin to think that our own spiritual journeys should be calm and comfortable, we must remember the wise men and their diligent expedition.

The Look: Since this is an Advent celebration, we once again incorporated an Advent candelabra into the display. To pick up the expedition theme, we created a display using backpacks of various sizes and materials, ropes, and boots. These items were placed alongside the communion elements.

Featured Option: Communion

Worship Celebration

Play a Christmas jazz CD; use pre-celebration lighting.

Opening Music

Band (Instrumental)   **"What Child Is This"**

Light band and project onscreen.

Call to Worship and Storytelling

Host and Storyteller   **"The Wise Men"**

Light speaker; project onscreen with two graphics (see script).

Christmastime gets us back in touch with many characters we may remember from childhood: Mary, Joseph, a baby, shepherds, an angel, and the wise men. You probably have some sort of visual picture in your head of what they all looked like. You may picture the wise men as three men wearing beautifully designed headwear trimmed with metallic thread. You might imagine that they were quiet and discreet gentlemen just wandering around looking for some way to spend their days, and who arrived at the manger, cool, calm and collected. (*Use self-created graphic stills of traditional wise men.*)

(*Project graphics onscreen*). Think again as you hear the wise men's story…

They arrived in Jerusalem shortly after Jesus' birth, determined to find the Christ child. King Herod caught wind of their determination, and felt extremely threatened by a baby who could cause such a stir. Herod gathered together the chief priests and scribes, and asked them where the Messiah was to be born. They told him that according to prophecy, the baby was to be born in Bethlehem. Herod immediately began scheming to get rid of this child. So he commissioned the wise men, the Ivy League scholars, to go find the child so that he could worship too. But who was he kidding? He wanted to do away with the little King.

So the wise persons set out, not on a Sunday stroll, but on a long and treacherous expedition (*show main graphic*) with only a star to guide them. Short on food, long on thirst, they crossed the seemingly endless miles across the desert. They were travel worn and weary: beards scruffy, fingernails dirty, shoes worn, hearts lonely for their loved ones back east. Then finally one night, they saw that the star had stopped. They found the place where the star hovered over, and they could hardly contain themselves. Overcome with emotion, they fell down to worship the child, Jesus.

Today our own Advent journey takes a different turn. What would it take to go totally out of our way on an expedition to God? How do you and I begin to focus all our energy and resources on being prepared to meet God?

Prayer

Host

Continue lighting as before; play soft music under. Project words of prayer.

Will you stand and join me in the response displayed on the screen? I will begin.

Leader: God, during this Advent we want to prepare ourselves for the journey, the diligent expedition.

People: Help us, Lord, to be ready.

Leader: Though you have created the world and are present and at work in it, the world doesn't acknowledge you. We, too, often fail to notice your presence.

People: Give us, Lord, eyes of faith so we may recognize you at work in the world around us.

Leader: You came to your own people, but were rejected.

People: We want you, Lord. Help us in this season of Advent to open ourselves to your coming.

Leader: And when we want you, and believe you are who you claim to be, you make us to be our true selves. Our child of God selves.

People: This is our need. Take our lives and make us ready for you. Amen.

Songs Celebration

Band **"Every Move I Make"**
"Open the Eyes of My Heart"
"O Come All Ye Faithful" (2 verses)

Light band; project words onscreen.

Announcements

Host

Light host; project speaker with graphics.

Offerings and Featured Music

Band **"Hands"**

Light band and project intermittently with graphic.

Message

Speaker   **"A Diligent Expedition"**

Light speaker; project graphics onscreen.

Communion

Host introduces

Light host.

When we take the bread and cup, we identify ourselves with Jesus Christ who first identified himself with us by becoming human, by being born in a manager in Bethlehem 2000 years ago. Eat this bread and drink this cup. Welcome the coming of Emmanuel, God with us!

Band   **"Cradle Prayer"**

Light band; project communion elements.

Sending Out

Host or Speaker

Light speaker; project graphic.

Exit Music

Band   **"What Child Is This"**

as before

Celebration

31

Uncommon Power

Felt Need: We need intimate connections to trust a humble Savior.

Desired Outcome: To take steps to begin trusting God and others

Theme: Uncommon Power

Word: Matthew 2:11

Metaphor/Image: Modern-day stark urban manger scene

The Lesson: The season of Advent allows the unique opportunity to consider the upside-down Kingdom. We climb the ladder of success, but God came down to us. We try to gain power, but God became vulnerable, gave up his power, and became human. This is a God who desires intimacy above control. People are drawn to a Savior like that. It's uncommon.

The Look: For the graphic, we arranged and photographed a modern-day manger scene. We found an old brick building in an alley, and placed a wooden crate for Jesus' manger at the doorway. We then added graffiti on the wall. We used the same crate for the stage display and added candle stands and our Advent candelabra. The additional option of Infant Baptism and or Dedication always creates a powerful Christmas Sunday experience.

Featured Option: Infant Dedication or Baptism

Worship Celebration

Play a Manheim Steamroller Christmas CD before celebration begins.
Use pre-celebration lighting.

Prelude

Kid's choir or Bell choir

Light choir; play on cue. Project choir onscreen; play live instrumental as they exit.

Opening Music

Band   **"Sweet Little Jesus Boy"**

Light band and end by projecting main graphic.

Call to Worship

Host and 3 vocalists   **"Uncommon Love"**

Light host and band; project main graphic throughout.

Host: When God opened heaven and sent his beloved Son into our world, God used a completely surprising and paradoxical strategy. One that you and I wouldn't think was reasonable for the God of the universe.

Vocal 1: He was born in a manger, not a mansion.

Vocal 2: While the religious looked for the Messiah in the synagogues,

Vocal 3: God showed up in the streets.

Host: Newborns should have clean, sanitary beds,

Vocal 1: But Jesus took his first breath amid dung and disease.

Vocal 2: Broken bottles.

Vocal 3: Broken lives.

Host: People like power. We work hard to climb the ladder of success and grasp for control.

Vocal 1: God came down.

Vocal 3: Gave up control.

Vocal 2: Became vulnerable.

Vocal 1: God in a baby.

Host: Christmas is about God's remarkable display of uncommon power and uncommon love. Let us lay down our lives to serve the One who served us.

164

Songs Celebration

Band   **"Can't Nobody"**
                                                     "Away in a Manger"

Light band; project words onscreen.

Infant Baptism or Dedication and Prayer

Host

Light speaker and altar area. Project baby picture, and graphic (dissolve between). Band softly plays under host; begin vocals when baptisms begin and resume instrumental for prayer.

In this final week of the Advent Season, we recognize the uncommon gift of God's Son, Jesus, and celebrate the new little lives that are among us this year. Something we do each year at Christmas time is to allow the opportunity for parents to offer their children to the Lord for baptism or dedication. We understand that these children truly belong to God, and trust that God will fulfill God's promise to them as we promise to raise them in homes that reflect Christ's presence. We pray for these children and rejoice with their families for the ongoing work of God in their lives.

(*To the parents*) As real followers of Jesus, I will ask you to state your commitment. Do you believe in the Bible as God's Word for our lives? (Yes) Have you claimed Jesus as Lord of your life? (Yes) Will you raise your child in a home that centers on Christ so that when they are old enough, they may be better prepared to claim Jesus as Lord for themselves? (Yes)

(*To the congregation*) Will you be an example to these children, providing them with a safe place to grow in that they see Christ in you? If so, answer "we do." (*We do.*)

We encourage extended families and friends to stand where you are when your child is being dedicated or baptized. Let's enjoy this time of celebration together.

Prayer

Let's bow our heads together:

Lord, these small miracles before us represent your best design: little hands that will do your work; small feet that will walk the Jesus journey; and soft hearts that will touch others with your love. Uncommon miracles. God, we pray for these parents, that they will be given the wisdom and the discipline they will need for the task of raising these children so that they know you. Place your hand of promise on these children and parents alike. We claim them for you.

Lord, we humble ourselves before you. You said we must come as little children: open, vulnerable, and trusting. Make our hearts childlike and loving. Lord, we celebrate your presence here today. Amen.

Band   **"Welcome to our World"**

Light participants and band; project participants onscreen if possible.

Announcements and Mission Moment

Host

Light host; project graphics. Consider using this time to talk about or show a video clip of a special Christmas outreach.

Offerings and Featured Music

Band   **Instrumental Christmas Medley**

Light band and project onscreen.

Message

Speaker   **"Uncommon Power"**

Light speaker and project onscreen with graphics.

Sending Out

Host

Light host; project main graphics.

In the Incarnation, God demonstrated uncommon power. God chose not a mansion, but a manger. To the world, this kind of power just doesn't make sense; it is foolish. But to those who grasp its beauty, their lives will be totally uncommon. Share the Christmas message this week. Amen.

Exit Music

Band   **"Sweet Little Jesus Boy"**

as before

Appendix A: Songs & Hymns

Song Title	Artist	Compact Disc	Label	WC#
Almighty	Wayne Watson	Home Free	Word Music	18
Amazing Grace	Ginghamsburg Band	The Felt Need	Ginghamsburg Church	12, 15
Another Day in Paradise	Phil Collins	Serious Hits . . . Live!	Atlantic	14
Arise, Shine	Steven Upspringer		Priesthood Publications	10
Away in a Manger		UM Hymnal #217		31
Awesome God	Rich Mullins	Awesome God	Edwards Grand Corp, Inc.	8
Can't Nobody Do Me Like Jesus	Andrae Crouch	Best of Andrae Crouch	Hal Leonard Music	16, 31
Carry Me High	Rebecca St. James	God	Forefront	24
Cats in the Cradle	Harry Chapin	Greatest Stories Live	Elektra	1
Celebrate Jesus	Arr. Francis Wyatt	The Felt Need	Ginghamsburg Church	20
Cheer's Theme Song	Bob James	Television's Greatest Hits—70's & 80's	TeeVee Toons	21
Come Just as You Are	Maranatha	Praise Classics: Lord of Lords	Word Entertainment	12
Come, Now is the Time	Brian Doerksen	UM Hymnal #328		4, 26
Cradle Prayer	Rebecca St. James	Christmas	Forefront	30
Create in Me a Clean Heart	Integrity Music	Perfect Peace	Integrity's Hosanna! Music	22
Crown Him With Many Crowns	Arr. Michael W. Smith	I'll Lead You Home	Reunion Records	14
Dance Like David (When the Spirit of the Lord)	Fred Hammond & RFC	Pages of Life, Chapters 1 & 2	BMG/Verity	24
Don't You Forget About Me	Simple Minds	Breakfast Club Soundtrack	A & M	19
Empty Hearts	The Kry	Unplugged	Malaco Records	7
Even God Must Get the Blues	JoDee Messina	I'm Alright	Atlantic	2
Every Breath You Take	Police	Greatest Hits	Polydor Records	18
Every Move I Make	Arr. Francis Wyatt	The Felt Need	Ginghamsburg Church	9, 10, 17, 18, 30
Faith of the Heart	Rod Stewart	Patch Adams Soundtrack	Universal Records	26
Feelin Groovy	Simon and Garfunkel	Greatest Hits	Columbia	1
Fragile	Sting	Very Best of Sting and Police	A & M	28
From This Moment	Shania Twain	Come on Over	Mercury Records	23

Song Title	Artist	Compact Disc	Label	WC#
Glory to Glory	Fred Hammond	Pages of Life	BMG/Verity	25, 27
God Is So Good	Arr. Francis Wyatt	The Felt Need	Ginghamsburg	1
Great Is Thy Faithfulness	Arr. Francis Wyatt	UM Hymnal #140		29
Hands	Jewel	Spirit	WEA/Atlantic	30
He Won't Let You Go	The Kry	Unplugged	Malaco Records	3, 11
Heaven Is in My Heart	Graham Kendrick	Highest Place	Integrity/Hosanna! Music	13, 15, 29
He'll Welcome Me	Brooklyn Tabernacle Choir	Favorite Song of All	WEA/Warner Bros.	13
Hold On (Help Is on the Way)	Whitney Houston	The Preacher's Wife Soundtrack	BMG/Arista	11
Hope to Carry On	Caedmon's Call	Caedmon's Call	Chordant	11
I Can't Stop Thinking About You	The Kry	Unplugged	Malaco Records	3, 4
I Could Sing of Your Love	Caedmon's Call	WOW 1998, Volume 2	Word Music	5, 8
I Go to Extremes	Billy Joel	Storm Front	Sony Music	24
I Go to the Rock	Whitney Houston	The Preacher's Wife Soundtrack	BMG/Arista	7
I Love to Praise Him	Miami Music Workshop	Jesus is the Real Thing	Pamplin Music	19
I Love You Lord	Laurie Klein	Exalt Him V.2	House of Mercy/Maranatha!Music	6
I Need You More	Hosanna	Revival at Brownsville	World Entertainers	4, 5, 7, 11, 20, 28
I See You	Michael W. Smith	Exodus	Rockettown Records	25, 27
I Still Haven't Found What I'm Looking For	U2	Joshua Tree	Chappel	13
I Surrender All	Arr. Francis Wyatt	The Felt Need	Ginghamsburg	22
I Walk by Faith	Arr. Francis Wyatt	The Felt Need	Ginghamsburg	11
I Want to Know What Love Is	Foreigner	The Very Best & Beyond	Atlantic	17
I Want to Thank You Lord	Maranatha	Praise Band 1-3	Pamplin Music	13
I Wish We'd All Been Ready	DC Talk	People Get Ready	Forefront Records	10
If I Ever Lose My Faith	Sting	Sting Hits	A & M	25
I'm Not Afraid	Brooklyn Tabernacle Choir	Praise Him Live	WEA/Warner Bros.	25
In Return	Bebe & Cece Winans	Bebe & Cece Winans	Quardant Dist. Group	16

168

Song Title	Artist	Compact Disc	Label	WC#
Keep the Rocks Silent	Babbie Mason	Praise Celebration	Sony/Word	19
Kind and Generous	Natalie Merchant	Ophelia	Elektra	12
Land of Confusion	Genesis	Invisible Touch	Atlantic	2
Lay Down Your Gods	The Kry	You	Freedom Records	14
Life Is a Highway	Tom Cochrane	Mad, Mad World	Capital EMI	29
Lord I Lift Your Name on High	Arr. Francis Wyatt	The Felt Need	Ginghamsburg	23
Love You So Much	Heritage Singers	You Are Holy	Chappel	6
Missing Persons	Michael W. Smith	Live the Life	Reunion Records	8
More Than You Know	Out of Eden	WOW 1998	EMI Christian Music	20
Name	Goo Goo Dolls	Boy Named Goo	WEA/Warner Brothers	23
Never Surrender	Corey Hart	Best of Corey Hart	Capital EMI	27
Nevertheless	GMWA Mass Choir	What He's Done For Me	MCG	27
New Song Arisin'	Darrell Evans	Let the River Flow	Integrity/Hosanna Music	1
Nothing but the Blood of Jesus	Arr. Francis Wyatt	The Felt Need	Ginghamsburg	2
Now Behold the Lamb	Kirk Franklin	Christmas	Gospocentric	2
O Come All Ye Faithful		UM Hymnal #234		30
O Come, O Come Emmanuel		UM Hymnal #211		29
Oh Lord, You're Beautiful	Keith Green	So You Want to Go Back to Egypt	Birdwing Music	1, 3
Open Arms	Journey	Greatest Hits	Sony/Columbia	27
Open the Eyes of My Heart	Paul Baloche	Because We Believe	Hosanna Music	7, 11 19, 30
Order My Steps	Brooklyn Tabernacle Choir	Favorite Song of All	WEA/Warner Bros.	15
People Get Ready	Crystal Lewis	People Get Ready	EMI Christian Music	29
Precious Lord		UM Hymnal #474		16
Revolution	The Beatles	Hey Jude	Capital EMI	16
Right Here, Right Now	Jesus Jones	Doubt	SBK Records	9

169

Song Title	Artist	Compact Disc	Label	WC#
Running on Empty	The Eagles	Greatest Hits	Elektra/Asylum Records	3
Seek First	Susan Ashton	Songs From the Loft	Reunion Records	3
Send Your Rain	Kelly Carpenter	Passion	Star Song Records	9
Shine on Us	Phillips, Craig and Dean	My Utmost for His Highest	Word Ent.	8, 15, 17, 21
Show Me the Way	Styx	Return to Paradise	CMC International Records	22
Sleeping Giant	Petra	Wake-Up Call	Word Music	10
Soon and Very Soon	Haven	Acapella	Haven Ministries	16
Song for Jesus (AKA Song for Mama)	Boyz 2 Men	Soulfood	BMG/Arista	20
Spread Love	Take 6	Take 6	Reprise	17
Starting Over	Reba McEntire	Starting Over	Universal/MCI	22
Step by Step	Audio Adrenaline	Forefront Records Birthday Album	Forefront	5, 6, 26
Still I Will Trust You	Brooklyn Tabernacle Choir	Favorite Song of All	WEA/Warner Brothers	4
Sunscreen	Baz Luhrmann	Something for Everybody	EMD/Capitol	21
Surely the Presence		UM Hymnal #328		3
Sweet Dreams	Eurythmics	Gratis Hits	Artisen/BMG	8
Sweet Little Jesus Boy	Rebecca St. James	Christmas	Forefront	31
Sweet Mercies	David Ruis	Passion	Star Song Records	12, 17, 22
Take My Life	Cindy Morgan	Best So Far	World Entertainers	18
The Long Run	Eagles	Greatest Hits Volume 2	Elektra	5
Time After Time	Calvin Hunt	Mercy Saw Me	Pamplin Music	15
Walk on Water	Eddie Money	Greatest Hits	Sony	26
We Fall Down	Chris Tomlin	Passion	Star Song Records	14, 24
Welcome to our World	Michael W. Smith	Christmastime		31
We've Come to Praise You	Michael James	Songs From the Loft	Reunion Records	21
What a Friend We Have in Jesus		UM Hymnal #526		15
What a Mighty God	Various	America's 25 Favorite Praise and Worship, Vol. 2	BMG/Brentwood Music	2, 17, 24
What Child Is This		UM Hymnal #219		30
What If	Reba McIntyre for the Salvation Army (1-song CD)		Star Struck Productions (MCA)	16

Song Title	Artist	Compact Disc	Label	WC#
What If I Stumble?	DC Talk	Jesus Freak	Forefront	28
What We've Come Here For	Michael W. Smith	Songs From the Loft	Reunion Records	21
What's Love Got to Do With It?	Tina Turner	Private Dancer	EMD/Capitol	6
Where Do I Go?	Ashley Cleveland/ Gary Chapman	Songs From the Loft	Reunion Records	12, 22, 28
Where He Leads Me	Twila Paris	My Utmost For His Highest	Sony/Word	9
Worship You	Don Moen	God Is Good	Hosanna Music	23
Yes, Lord	John Kee	Yes, Lord	Providence Distributors	23
You Alone	Wayne & Libby Huirua	Worship Leader, Volume 15	Worship Leader	14, 28
You Are God	Scott Underwood	Worship Leader, Volume 4	Worship Leader	23
You Don't Count the Cost	Billy Dean	Greatest Hits	EMD/Capitol	6

171

Appendix B: Video Titles & Sources

Video Title	Scene/Portion	WC#	Available From:
	Footage of whitewater rafting	3	Local library
Braveheart	No specific clip.	27	Video rental store
The Century: America's Time With Peter Jennings	Scenes depicting violence like the assassination attempts on the lives of Ronald Regan and George Wallace.	2	Video rental store
City Slickers	Scene where Billy Crystal's character tells Daniel Stern's character that even though he has messed up his whole life, "We all get a do-over."	22	Video rental store
Contact	Scene where Jodie Foster's character is sitting in the space capsule. She is afraid, yet says over and over, "I'm OK to go; I'm OK to go."	13	Video rental store
Highlights '97	Testimony of Carolyn Slaughter talking about her marriage.	4	www.ginghamsburg.org
Hook	Scene where Grandmother Wendy asks Peter, "What's so terribly important about your terribly important life?"	1	Video rental store
Indiana Jones and the Last Crusade	**Clip 1:** Scene where Indy and his father are looking at the diary they found, and are musing over the meaning of the phrases "the breath of God," "the path of God," and "the word of God." **Clip 2:** Scene where Indy says, "May he who illuminated this book illuminate me." **Clip 3:** Scene where Indy steps out to cross the canyon, and a footbridge mysteriously appears.	15	Video rental store
It's a Wonderful Life	Scene at the end where George exclaims, "It's a wonderful life!"	10	Video rental store
Jerry McGuire	Scene where Jerry writes his mission statement, shows it to his boss, and then is fired.	28	Video rental store
Malcolm X	Scene where Malcolm, in a small chapel setting, articulately explains his faith to the presiding clergyman.	19	Video rental store
Media Resource '99	"Kids Say Thanks"	26	www.ginghamsburg.org
Media Resource '99	"Braveheart" animation	27	www.ginghamsburg.org
Media Resource '99	"Kids Say Thanks": scene where a child says, "My teacher told me that it's OK to be scared."	28	www.ginghamsburg.org
MSWII Resource	Etch-A-Sketch animation	22	www.ginghamsburg.org
MSWII Resource	"God in Me" animation	5	www.ginghamsburg.org
MSWII Resource	"The Good Life"	7	www.ginghamsburg.org
MSWII Resource	On the Campus: "What's It Mean to Love Someone"	6	www.ginghamsburg.org
MSWII Resource	On the Campus: "What's It Mean to Love God"	6	www.ginghamsburg.org
River Wild	Scene at the end of the wild ride where Meryl Streep and her family are silently hurtling downstream.	3	Video rental store
Shadowlands	Scene where C.S. Lewis is giving a lecture and says, "Pain is God's megaphone to rouse a deaf world."	11	Video rental store
Shawshank Redemption	Scene where Morgan Freeman talks about pain while sitting on the bleachers in the prison yard.	2	Video rental store
Summer Vacation	Scene where the Griswold family returns, drives into the garage, and the luggage on top of the car is knocked off.	29	Video rental store
The Visual Edge	On the Street: "What Does Jesus Look Like?"	19	www.cokesbury.com
The Visual Edge	On the Street: "Why Church?"	25	www.cokesbury.com
The Visual Edge	"Walk on Water" animation	26	www.cokesbury.com
The Visual Edge	"Pentecost—In Your Dreams"	8	www.cokesbury.com
The Visual Edge	"The Idea"	9	www.cokesbury.com
The Visual Edge	"The Jump"	9	www.cokesbury.com
Wizard of Oz	Scene where Lion says that he wants to get courage from the Wizard.	24	Video rental store